SHERMAN INVADES GEORGIA

An Association of the U.S. Army Book

SHERMAN INVADES GEORGIA

Planning the North Georgia Campaign
Using a Modern Perspective

JOHN R. SCALES

NAVAL INSTITUTE PRESS
Annapolis, Maryland

Naval Institute Press
291 Wood Road
Annapolis, MD 21402

Library of Congress Cataloging-in-Publication Data

Scales, John R.
Sherman invades Georgia / John R. Scales.
    p. cm.
Includes bibliographical references and index.
ISBN 1-59114-815-4 (alk. paper)
1. Atlanta Campaign, 1864. 2. Sherman, William T. (William Tecumseh), 1820-1891—Military leadership. I. Title.
E476.7.S325 2006
973.7'371—dc22
                    2006015638

Printed in the United States of America on acid-free paper ∞

12 11 10 09 08 07 06 05   9 8 7 6 5 4 3 2
First printing

Interior design and composition: Chris Onrubia, Fineline Graphics

*To infantrymen,
who die when generals fail
their war on the map.*

Contents

PART 2. ESTIMATE OF THE SITUATION

PART 3. THE REST OF THE STORY

Figures

Photographs

Maps

Tables

Preface

THE ATLANTA CAMPAIGN OF 1864 was one of the most interesting and important campaigns of the American Civil War. At its beginning, the Confederate Army in the West—the Army of Tennessee—was strong and capable, though outnumbered. By the end of the campaign, the Army of Tennessee had been forced to evacuate Atlanta and could neither attack the Union Army successfully nor protect the agricultural center of Georgia. The Union Army had occupied northern Georgia and the city of Atlanta, the rail hub of the Confederacy. Major General William Tecumseh Sherman, the Union commander, had accomplished this result with relatively few casualties, using his superior numbers to maneuver the Confederate Army from successive strong positions. The choices he faced at the beginning of the campaign are the subject of this book.

PURPOSE

I intend for this book to serve two audiences: military professionals, and persons interested in seeing one of the premier campaigns of the Civil War from a new perspective.

First, military commanders and staff will be able to use it for study and as a source book. Military units often conduct "staff rides," the purpose of which is to train the unit staff by using a real military battle or campaign as a vehicle for study. To facilitate this usage, I laid out the book in chapters that follow the format of an "estimate of the situation," a logical decision-making process formulated in modern times. The estimate of the situation is a clear exposition of the planning factors that a commander should consider before making a deliberate decision—a decision for which he or she has the luxury of time to weigh alternatives and to make detailed plans. It is similar to, but not identical with, the "Military Decision-Making Process" that evolved from the commander's estimate. The following table is an outline of the commander's estimate.[1] Later in the book are blank forms for readers who might desire to formulate or evaluate their own approaches using the estimate format. However, it should be understood that Civil War commanders did not use the estimate-of-the-situation process for decision making at all because the process had not been invented yet. Their decisions were taken in an informal and often undocumented manner.

Another purpose of the book is to provide a different perspective of the campaign to the Civil War buff or interested layman. By using a modern planning format and explaining the unavoidable military jargon, I hope to make very complex matters a little more understandable. Additionally, I

TABLE 1 *Estimate of the Situation Outline*

1. Mission
2. The situation and courses of action
   A. Situation analysis
       1.   Geostrategic context
          (a) Domestic and international context
          (b) Characteristics of the operational area
       2.   Analysis of the enemy
          (a) Broad courses of action
          (b) Political and military intentions and objectives
          (c) Military strategic and operational advantages and limitations
          (d) Possible external military support
          (e) Centers of gravity
          (f) Specific operational characteristics (strength, composition, location and disposition, reinforcements, logistics, time and space factors, and combat efficiency)
       3.   Friendly situation—same factors as used for enemy
       4.   Assumptions
       5.   Deductions—relative combat power
   B. Course of action development
       1.   Attack
       2.   Defend
       3.   Retrograde
       4.   Reinforce
3. Analysis of opposing courses of action
4. Comparison of own courses of action
5. Decision

limited the information in the book as far as possible to that information possessed by General Sherman, as documented in his correspondence during the campaign, not in his after-the-fact reports and autobiography. In this way I hope to give the reader a sense of the uncertainty that real commanders must face. This approach is in contrast to that used by modern historians and armchair strategists, who have all the records of both sides at hand.

One thing this book is not is a definitive history of the campaign. Participants and historians have written many volumes about it and new books appear periodically. A listing of some of these appears in the reference section.

ORGANIZATION

The book is organized into three distinct parts, each part containing several chapters. Each chapter has footnotes with supplementary information and endnotes containing sources. Additionally, the book's supplementary materials include a list of references for those who wish to pursue further research, a glossary, an appendix suggesting how to use the book for a military staff ride, and an explanation of military map symbols as used in the illustrations.

The first part of the book, chapters 1 through 4, constitutes a brief introduction to the Civil War and operational art. It also describes the strategic picture and acquaints the reader with Civil War organizations and techniques. Even readers with extensive knowledge of the campaign will find the section valuable in setting the stage.

The second part, chapters 5 through 11, is the most important. Placed in the perspective of late April 1864, just prior to the opening of the campaign, it develops an "estimate of the situation" that General Sherman might have formed at the beginning of the campaign, had he been a modern general. This part is based on the facts available to him then. In each of these chapters the reader is given the information available to General Sherman and general guidelines as to what a modern military planner would do with that information. Immediately after each set of guidelines are blank forms that the reader can use to formulate his or her own estimate. The final section of each chapter presents my "school solution"—one element of a possible estimate of the situation. Additionally, the section gives what General Sherman thought—if I could find any evidence of it.

The last part of the book, chapters 12 through 14, contains a brief description of the actual situation (as opposed to the perceived situation) and what happened when General Sherman executed his plan. The controversies surrounding the actions of generals and their subordinates—frequent in this campaign as in every other Civil War campaign—are listed but not emphasized. The section illustrates that "no plan survives contact with the enemy."

FOCUS

A real difference between this book and most similar books is its concentration on campaign planning rather than on one or more battles. In military terms, the book deals with planning, not execution, and with the "operational" level of war rather than the tactical level or the strategic level.* I emphasize the "art of war on the map," to use Jomini's term, as opposed to the war on the ground.² The reader will find little discussion of individual engagements or even of the movements of specific units. Studying Civil War battles can be very interesting and informative, but their direct relevance to modern combat is limited. On the other hand, the planning and conduct of an entire Civil War campaign can have pertinent lessons for modern military commanders and planners.

---

* Current military thought defines the three levels of war as strategy, operational art, and tactics. Quoting *The Joint Officer's Staff Guide* (Armed Forces Staff College, 1993), the strategic level of war is "the level of war at which a nation or group of nations determines national or alliance security objectives and develops and uses national resources to accomplish those objectives. Actions at this level establish national and alliance military objectives; sequence initiatives; define limits and assess risks for the use of military and other instruments of power; develop global or theater war plans to achieve those objectives; and provide armed forces and other capabilities in accordance with the strategic plan" (I-39). The tactical level of war is that "at which battles and engagements are planned and executed to accomplish military objectives assigned to tactical units or task forces. Activities at this level focus on the ordered arrangement and maneuver of combat elements in relation to each other and to the enemy to achieve combat objectives" (I-41). The operational level is that "at which campaigns and major operations are planned, conducted, and sustained to accomplish strategic objectives within theaters or areas of operations. Activities at this level link tactics and strategy by establishing operational objectives needed to accomplish the strategic objectives, sequencing events to achieve the operational objectives, initiating actions, and applying resources to bring about and sustain these events. These activities imply a broader dimension of time and space than do tactics; they ensure the logistics and administrative support of tactical forces, and provide the means by which tactical successes are exploited to achieve strategic objectives" (I-32). Quoting General (retired) Glenn K. Otis in his essay included in the U.S. Army Center for Military History's *On Operational Art*, ". . . strategy wins the war, operational art aims at winning the campaigns that support the strategy, and tactics win battles in the campaigns" (Newell and Krause, 1994).

The decision to concentrate on General Sherman's point of view (with apologies to my ancestors, uniformly Confederate) is dictated by his preponderance of combat power and possession of a clear mission coupled with wide latitude in execution. He had enough freedom of action to provide the scope for us to fully explore the modern campaign planning process.

Like much of the rest of book, the conclusions and lessons are mine. Analyses and the "school solutions" given are my opinions—feel free to disagree with them. They will have served their purpose if they provide fuel for further thought. If you enjoy the book and learn a little from it, its primary purpose will have been served.

ACKNOWLEDGMENTS

Several of my colleagues assisted me in the preparation of this book. Army Colonel (now retired) Bob Butto, a companion senior service college fellow at the Center for Strategic and International Studies (CSIS), made several valuable suggestions. Mike Cantagallo, a CSIS intern, performed much useful research as well as other chores. The other military fellows, particularly Marine Colonel (now retired) Sam Hall, provided a great deal of encouragement as well. My friends and relatives Michele Wassel Hood and Becky and Warren Gaylord gave me meals and a place to stay during my battlefield wanderings. My family also greatly encouraged me, putting up with frequent physical and mental absences. My mother-in-law, the late Mrs. Louis Gaylord, was very helpful in proofing an early draft and my son Richard practiced his driving by chauffeuring me around the area.

Special thanks go to Mr. John A. Hixson of Fort Leavenworth (my apologies for not knowing his rank) who made some very insightful and helpful comments on the original manuscript and pointed out useful avenues of inquiry and references.

Much of the credit goes to those soldiers, sailors, airmen, and Marines with whom I served for over 32 years. Their patriotism, ability, and enthusiasm were key to any success I experienced and any lessons I learned.

Of course, the responsibility for any errors is mine alone.

END-OF-CHAPTER NOTES

1. Joint Pub 3-0, *Doctrine for Joint Operations* (Washington, D.C.: U.S. Government Printing Office, 1 February 1995), B1–B3.
2. Baron Antoine Henri Jomini, *Summary of the Art of War* (New York: G. P. Putnam, 1854), 79.

SHERMAN INVADES GEORGIA

Part One
The Civil War and Operational Art

CHAPTER 1

Organizations and Operations in the Civil War

T his chapter gives background information on the organizations used during the American Civil War and the types of operations conducted at the tactical and operational levels. Included are illustrations of the specific organizations of the Union and Confederate armies, from corps level down to companies, including the roles of the infantry, the artillery, and the cavalry. Succeeding sections cover types of operations: offensive, defensive, and retrograde.

ORGANIZATIONS

In 1864 the basic independent war-fighting entity of both the Union and the Confederacy was the field army. An army, usually made up of several army corps and with an aggregate strength ranging from 30,000 men to more than 100,000 men, was expected to campaign and fight battles against its counterpart on the other side. By this time, the military of each side had evolved away from the separate small units that had made up the regular army and the militia, typically companies of fewer than 100 men or regiments of fewer than 1,000 men. Each side now deployed complete field armies made up of army corps, modeled on those of the Napoleonic Wars fought in Europe fifty years previously.

Units

Each army corps had from two to four divisions, each encompassing 3,000 to 8,000 men, for a typical corps strength from 10,000 to more than 20,000 soldiers. Corps in the Union Army were assigned Roman numerals, and those in the Confederate Army were named for their commanders. A corps could be expected to operate independently a distance away from the rest of the army, but not so far away that it could be cut off and destroyed by a greatly superior force of the enemy. Each corps would usually have assigned to it one or more roads upon which to move and deploy.

Figures 1.1 through 1.6 show the basic organizational structures of typical Civil War armies (circa 1864) and their modern map symbols. The list of map symbols at the end of this book explains modern military map symbols in more detail.

Figures 1.1 through 1.6 show several differences between the Union and Confederate sides. Two of those differences are the ranks of the higher-ranking officers—the entire Union Army having only one lieutenant general, Ulysses S. Grant, and no full generals—and the allocation of artillery, to division level in the Union Army and to corps level in the Confederate Army. The focus of this book is the army group (the modern term for a collection of field armies deployed under a single commander directed toward a common purpose)—field army—army corps level of command, so these and other minor differences are not addressed.

Infantry

*The infantry was the decisive arm, forming the mass of the army. It carried the burden of the attack and the defense. Although the other arms played an important role, as outlined later in this chapter, in general neither artillery nor cavalry could stand alone against enemy infantry.**

Civil War armies were infantry armies. Most soldiers carried muzzle-loading, single-shot rifles (sometimes smoothbore muskets or, rarely, repeating rifles), marched on foot, and fought in ranks facing identically organized infantry lines on the other side. Of the effective soldiers present in General William Tecumseh Sherman's command on April 30, 1864, more than 80 percent were infantrymen. More than 6 percent were artillerymen, more than 7 percent were cavalry, and the rest were engineers and headquarters staff. Engineers were often infantrymen detailed to the task (see photo 1.1).

---

* There were exceptions. For example, at Malvern Hill in 1862, McClellan's artillery defeated an attack by Lee's infantry. During the war there were a few instances where well-led or well-armed (repeating rifles) dismounted cavalrymen, fighting as infantry, were able to defeat infantry.

Figure 1.1 *Field Army*

Commander:	Major General (Union Army)
	General (Confederate Army)
Made up of:	2 to 7 infantry corps
XXXX	36 to 50 cannon artillery reserve
⊠	1 cavalry corps (4,000 to 10,000 men)
	Engineer, logistic, and other such units
	30,000 to more than 100,000 men total

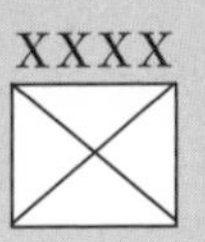

Figure 1.2 *Infantry Corps*

Commander:	Major General (Union Army)
	Lieutenant General (Confederate Army)
Made up of:	2 to 4 infantry divisions
XXX	10,000 to 25,000 men total
⊠	Confederate Army only:
	6 to 12 artillery batteries
	36 to 48 cannon total

Figure 1.3 *Infantry Division*

Commander:	Major General or Brigadier General
Made up of:	2 to 4 infantry brigades
XX	3,000 to 8,000 men total
⊠	Union Army only:
	2 artillery batteries
	12 cannon total

Figure 1.4 *Infantry Brigade*

Commander:	Brigadier General or Colonel
Made up of:	2 to 9 infantry regiments
X	800 to 3,000 men total

FIGURE 1.5 *Infantry Regiment*

Commander:	Colonel
Made up of:	10 infantry companies
	150 to 1,000 men total
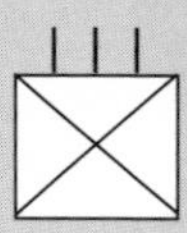	Photo 1.2 shows a Union infantry regiment.

FIGURE 1.6 *Infantry Company*

Commander:	Captain
Made up of:	15 to 100 men
	Note: The battalion, in modern armies an intermediate organization between company and regiment, was in the Civil War an ad hoc infantry unit of two or more companies, regimental size or smaller, organized for battle.

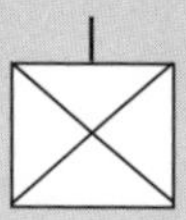

Field Artillery

Field artillery units contained two types of cannons: rifled and smoothbore. A rifled cannon firing a shell or solid shot was more accurate than a smoothbore but had a slower rate of fire. Rifled cannon were used against opposing artillery or other point targets. Smoothbore cannon, often firing heavy shot like a large shotgun, were particularly effective at short range against infantry. Unlike modern artillery, which is employed primarily in an indirect fire role, both rifled and smoothbore artillery were employed as direct-fire weapons—that is, against targets that could be seen by the cannoneers. Photo 1.3 depicts an artillery battery. During the Civil War, field artillery was used in a way similar to how modern machine guns are used.

Heavy artillery, including mortars and siege artillery, was used only rarely during mobile warfare, because of the large amount of transportation and logistics support required.

During an offensive operation, artillery concentrated direct fire on a particular target, usually opposing artillery or dense infantry formations, to suppress that target.

While defending, artillery was posted on the flanks of the infantry to deliver enfilade fire (along the line of the enemy), potentially causing more casualties than fire through the depth of the attacking line.

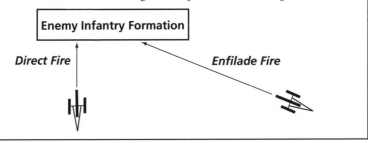

Cavalry

Cavalry was employed for scouting, discovering the enemy while protecting friendly forces from surprise. Due to its superior mobility, cavalry was also used to conduct raids against the enemy's supply lines.

Barring surprise, mounted cavalry could not successfully fight against opposing infantry and had to dismount (using a significant fraction of their manpower as horse holders) if they were to be effective. Photo 1.4 shows a Union cavalry regiment.

Sherman's Organization

In the North Georgia campaign, General Sherman controlled the entire Military Division (an administrative entity, not to be confused with the division itself, a tactical unit) of the Mississippi. The Military Division included three field armies in the Chattanooga, Tennessee, area, although one was really just a corps plus some cavalry. The Military Division also included other troops scattered throughout the Mississippi Basin in places such as Vicksburg, Mississippi; Memphis, Tennessee; Cairo, Illinois; and Nashville, Tennessee. Sherman let his rear headquarters in Nashville

Photo 1.1 *The 21st Michigan Infantry Regiment, stationed near Chattanooga. It was engaged in engineer duty, building bridges, erecting storehouses, etc., until June 11, 1864, and then at Lookout Mountain building hospitals, running mills, etc., until September 20.* Photo ARC 525071, National Archives, data from http://www.civilwararchive.–com/Unreghst/unmiinf3

control all these other troops, although he had to spend part of his time each day issuing instructions and handling routine matters brought to his attention by his subordinates. However, the bulk of his time was spent controlling his three field armies in operations against the Confederate Army in Georgia. In modern terms, Sherman was an army group commander. He issued orders to his three army commanders, coordinating their operations toward a single objective.

OPERATIONS

There are three classic types of operations: offensive, defensive, and retrograde.

- **Offensive** operations take the initiative, seizing territory and defeating the enemy's army.

- **Defensive** operations defeat an attack, gain time, retain territory, and allow forces to be concentrated elsewhere.
- **Retrograde** operations trade space for time, allowing the enemy to gain territory but penalizing the gain when possible. Retrograde operations are used when the enemy is so strong that a defense would be unsuccessful. Sometimes retrograde operations are considered a form of defense.

Although details of execution differ over time, the basic forms of each operation as practiced in the Civil War—or today—would be recognizable to Alexander the Great.

Offensive

Offensive operations—attacks—come in six forms: envelopment, frontal attack, infiltration, penetration, raid, and turning movement. The investment or siege of a fortified position sometimes is considered a seventh form of offensive combat. Civil War armies used all forms, although

PHOTO 1.2 *An unidentified Union infantry regiment formed in front of its camp, probably in Virginia. Note the mounted field officers, the band on formation's left (our right), and the regimental trains (wagons) to the rear.* PHOTO ARC 524905, NATIONAL ARCHIVES

infiltration was normally employed only as a raider's tactic. Forms of the attack are described and illustrated on the following pages. In each illustration, the attack is indicated by arrows.

 FRONTAL ATTACK. *The frontal attack is usually the least desirable form of attack, as it pits the attacker directly against the defender's strength. It is, however, the simplest offensive operation to execute and may be adopted if the enemy is weak or planning time is short.*

A famous example of a successful frontal attack (see figure above) occurred at Chattanooga in November 1863. The Union Army of the Cumberland was ordered to attack Missionary Ridge, east of town. The Confederate positions appeared strong and the attack was intended to be merely a diversion, while large forces attempted to envelop the Confederate flanks (figure 1.7). However, the Confederate trenches were poorly sited. Defenders in them could not see or shoot at attackers

PHOTO 1.3 *A Civil War artillery battery deployed near Ringgold, Georgia. The guns are deployed much closer together than they normally would be (usual interval 25 to 50 paces).* PHOTO ARC 524783, NATIONAL ARCHIVES

climbing the ridge, except in a few places. Also, the defender's fire was inhibited because their pickets (soldiers posted in front of the main line to provide early warning) were retreating from their positions. They were, therefore, just in front of the attacking force, and the Confederates wanted at all costs to avoid firing into their own men.

The Union attackers closed with the Confederate positions before more than one effective volley could be fired. Confederate reserves had been moved to meet the envelopment on the right, and were thus unavailable to restore the position. Most of the Confederate Army then broke and ran after their first volley to avoid being cut off and captured. Lieutenant Arthur MacArthur, father of General of the Army Douglas MacArthur (of World War II and Korean War fame), was awarded the Medal of Honor leading his regiment in this attack.

An equally famous example, this time of a failed frontal attack, occurred at Fredericksburg, Virginia, in December 1862 (see figure 1.8). Union Major General Ambrose Burnside ordered a frontal attack against General Robert E. Lee's strongly posted army, resulting in the loss of almost three Union soldiers to every Confederate casualty, in spite of Burnside's much greater numbers. His superior artillery—more guns on higher ground—controlled the river, the town, and most of the flood plain, allowing his army to cross over and form up for the attack. However, Confederate positions on and at the base of the hills above town were out of effective artillery range and his army was slaughtered trying to cross the open ground between the town and the hills.

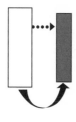

SINGLE ENVELOPEMENT. *A single envelopment concentrates the main attacking force against the side (flank) of the defender's position, while holding the defender's attention with a supporting attack or diversion. There are two advantages to attacking a flank: (1) The defender may not be ready for an attack there and is liable to be surprised or even panicked, and (2) the attacker can concentrate a relatively large force against the small number of defenders on the flank.*

Perhaps the most famous envelopment (see figure above) in the Civil War occurred at Chancellorsville, Virginia, in May 1863. General Lee, outnumbered more than two-to-one, found the Union right flank "in air" (unprotected; see figure 1.9) and dispatched Lieutenant General Thomas J. "Stonewall" Jackson (one of his two corps commanders) to attack it.

In an attack that cost him his life, Jackson enveloped and crushed the Union XI Corps, commanded by Major General Oliver Howard, leading to the demoralization and defeat of Major General Joseph Hooker's Union Army. The dense woods had concealed the Confederate weaknesses, and Hooker, who had sent most of his cavalry on an abortive raid toward Richmond and thus had little reconnaissance capability, lost confidence in his army and his plan. He ordered a withdrawal.

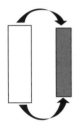

DOUBLE ENVELOPMENT. *A double envelopment is two attacks, one on either flank of the enemy. An attacker conducts an envelopment to avoid the defender's strength, but does so at the cost of increased complexity in planning and execution.*

The double envelopment (see figure above) is perhaps the most difficult offensive maneuver of all to execute. A successful battle of this sort is also called a "Cannae," after the famous Punic War battle. On the second day of Gettysburg, General Lee attempted a double envelopment, directing Lieutenant General Richard Ewell's corps to attack the Union right flank at Culp's Hill and Lieutenant General James Longstreet's corps to attack the Union left flank (figure 1.10). Due to several factors (not the least of which was Longstreet's reluctance to attack at all!), both efforts ended up being tactically frontal attacks, and both failed. Longstreet's attack failed when Brigadier General Governeur Warren, Major General George G. Meade's chief engineer, saw the danger to the Union left flank and on his own initiative ordered two brigades of the V Corps, in reserve, to occupy Little Round Top. Colonel Strong Vincent's brigade—Colonel Joshua Chamberlain's famous 20th Maine was one of his regiments—arrived just in time to halt the attack of Brigadier General Evander Law's brigade, which was on Longstreet's far right.*

A good example of a different type of operation, the penetration, occurred at Chickamauga, Georgia, in September 1863 (figure 1.11). Confederate General Braxton Bragg, his army reinforced by elements of two divisions

---

* For those Civil War trivia buffs who recognize my last name, Confederate Brigadier General Alfred M. Scales, wounded on the first day at Gettysburg while commanding a brigade of Pender's Division, A. P. Hill's Corps, Army of Northern Virginia, was not a direct ancestor, but rather a cousin of the author's great-great-grandfather.

INFILTRATION. *Infiltration is also a method used to avoid the defender's strength, but in this case the attacker attempts to do so by covert movement in small bodies, often in terrain offering concealment. Infiltration is very difficult to coordinate. It was seldom used in the Civil War, except by raiders who bypassed enemy armies in an attempt to destroy their supplies or transportation.*

PENETRATION. *Penetration is a variant of the frontal attack, except that rather than attacking across the front, the attacker concentrates his combat power in a narrow area and attempts to break that front, then spread out. It is essentially a frontal attack that seeks to create a flank to be enveloped within the defender's position.*

from Virginia under Longstreet, ordered a frontal attack. The unit on the Confederate far right flank was to start the attack and other units were to attack in turn as the unit on their right moved. The attack was unsuccessful (except in causing the Union Army to reinforce its left and weaken its right) until it reached an area where Major General John Bell Hood had massed his units in a column of brigades for the attack.

Coincidentally, at that point the Union commander, Major General William Rosecrans, had just moved a division out of the line by mistake. The brigades penetrated this weak point and routed the right flank of the Union Army. However, the Union left flank under Major General George Thomas (the "Rock of Chickamauga"), posted on strong terrain with flank protection, was able to hold until dark before retreating to Chattanooga.

Bombardment, starvation, mining (digging tunnels under enemy lines and placing explosives there), and building trenches (parallels) closer and closer to the defense—to cut down on the casualties of the attackers if an assault proves unavoidable—are the hallmarks of a siege (see page 14). Communications trenches—known as saps—connect the successive trench lines and provide the covered approach used to construct the next parallel. Saps and parallels were sited so that the enemy could not fire along the length of the trench from his positions ("enfilade fire"). A siege is slow and costly, but Civil War commanders considered its outcome—the defeat of the defender—to be almost inevitable. Considering how two

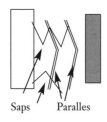

Saps   Paralles

SIEGE. *Little movement characterizes a siege or investment of a fortified position. The defenders may or may not be surrounded, but their fortifications are too strong for direct attack without extensive preparations.*

objective

TURNING MOVEMENT. *The antithesis of the siege is the turning movement. Sun Tzu said, "Supreme excellence consists in breaking the enemy's resistance without fighting." The turning movement is designed to do just that, by avoiding the defender's position and taking a point deep in his rear, through which his supplies and reinforcements must pass.*

famous Civil War sieges—Vicksburg* and Petersburg—turned out, they were almost certainly correct.

The turning movement (see figure above) may cause the defender to abandon his position, either to attack the attacker or to retreat. The defending soldiers are often upset by their direct route home being cut—the cry of "We're surrounded!" can induce panic even in experienced soldiers—and lose confidence in their commander, wondering, "How could he be fooled like this?" The effectiveness of the turning movement illustrates the importance of the psychological aspects of warfare. After all, the attacker usually exposes his own lines of communication to attack as well, yet the shock of his unexpected appearance in the rear often unhinges the defender.

Civil War commanders often attempted to turn their opponent's position, but sometimes did not succeed because the opponent was too alert. A famous successful turning movement precipitated the battle of Second Manassas (or Second Bull Run) in Virginia in August 1862 (figure 1.12). General Lee took his army, led by Lieutenant General Jackson's Corps, around Major General John Pope's Union army—using the Rappahannock River and the Bull Run Mountains to hide his movements—and seized Manassas Junction, a large Union supply depot.

---

* Private Samuel Hathcock, Company C, 41st Tennessee, CSA, the author's great-great-grandfather, was mortally wounded at the battle of Raymond during the campaign leading up to the siege of Vicksburg.

Photo 1.4. *An unidentified Union cavalry regiment has just crossed the Rappahannock River in Virginia on a pontoon bridge.* Photo ARC 524925–National Archives

Pope, confused and anxious to restore his supply lines, retreated from his advanced positions and attacked Jackson. Lee waited until Pope was fully engaged in attacking Jackson, then enveloped Pope's left with Longstreet's Corps, routing Pope's army.*

The raid is a form of attack similar to a turning movement. There is one important distinction. In a turning movement, the attacking army has adequate supplies and supply lines to sustain itself until the enemy army must act. In a raid, the attacking army—or more often a portion of the army—cannot adequately sustain itself behind enemy lines and must either quickly defeat the enemy's army or move to a place where supplies can reach it. Raiding by cavalry and by entire armies was frequent during the Civil War. A famous example was Lee's Gettysburg campaign (not the battle itself but the events leading up to the battle). Lee had to fight or retreat when encountering Meade's army rather than await attack because he did not

---

* Lieutenant John Green Guice, Company E, 4th Alabama, CSA, the author's great-grandfather, was severely wounded (for the third time—lieutenants have notoriously poor survivability) and permanently disabled while participating in Longstreet's attack.

FIGURE 1.7 *Battle of Missionary Ridge*

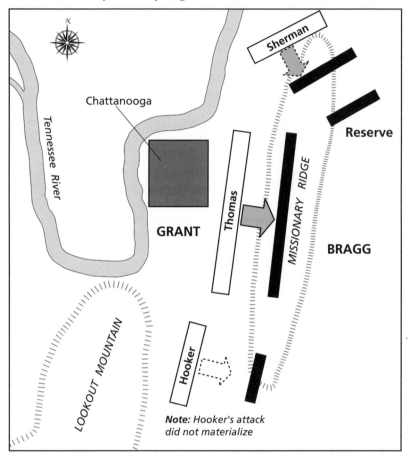

have enough food in his wagons to sustain his army. Lee's army could not forage in the presence of Meade's forces, because food collection required his units to spread out, leaving isolated units as easy pickings. Meade had railroad connections to his supply bases, and thus plenty of food.

Another example of an attempted turning movement becoming a raid was the Perryville campaign in the fall of 1862 (figure 1.13). General Bragg marched north from Chattanooga, bypassing the defenses of Nashville and moving into Kentucky, where he hoped to find supplies and a sympathetic populace. He planned to join General Edmund Kirby Smith's forces from Knoxville and threaten Union supply lines, rail lines leading south from Cincinnati and Louisville. His movement did cause Union Major General Don Carlos Buell's army to retrace its steps from

FIGURE 1.8 *Battle of Fredericksburg*

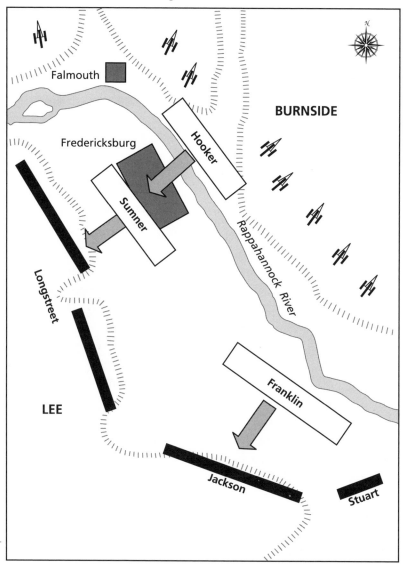

the vicinity of Huntsville, Alabama, all the way back into Kentucky to drive him out, but because of a less sympathetic reception than desired, a failed linkup with Kirby Smith, and a drawn battle at Perryville, Bragg was unable to sustain his maneuver. Running out of supplies and confidence, he retreated to Murfreesboro, Tennessee.

FIGURE 1.9 *Battle of Chancellorsville*

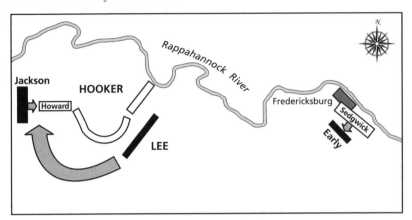

Modern examples of many of these offensive operations can be found in Operation Desert Storm, the liberation of Kuwait in 1991. At the conclusion of the air campaign, General H. Norman Schwarzkopf attacked across a broad front with his ground forces. His preponderance of strength allowed him to perform several offensive operations nearly simultaneously (a feint by the Marines from the Gulf, a supporting frontal attack by Marines and the Arab armies, an envelopment by the U.S. VII Corps, and a turning movement by the U.S. XVIII Airborne Corps). Figure 1.14 illustrates these operations against the familiar map of the Kuwait theater of operations.

It is interesting to note that the Iraqi high command did not expect either the envelopment or the turning movement, because they believed that it was impossible to move or supply large formations of soldiers that deep in the desert. The Global Positioning System (GPS) allowed the Allies to keep themselves oriented, find each other, and resupply the soldiers and vehicles. GPS was a technological surprise to the Iraqis. The Allied air campaign had blinded Iraqi sensors. Deception operations, including dummy radio traffic and extensive television coverage of Marine Corps amphibious rehearsals, led them to believe that all the Allied major units were still opposite their own front-line positions—shown as a heavy black line in the figure—or preparing for an amphibious assault.

Defensive

In contrast to the variety of offensive approaches, Civil War commanders used only a single form of defense. They might choose to entrench or

FIGURE 1.10 *Battle of Gettysburg*

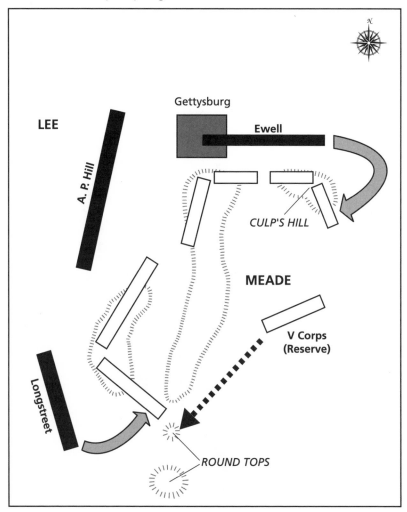

not—in 1864 they usually did—yet the form of the defense was the same in either case. The army would be posted on high ground if possible, with its flanks protected from envelopment by terrain barriers such as rivers, swamps, dense forest, steep hillsides, or similar obstacles (figure 1.15). The infantry and artillery would be deployed linearly, with a strong force—a reserve—sheltered behind the line to help any unit being overwhelmed or to replace units that were out of ammunition or badly hurt. The reserve could also counterattack the attacker if he should

FIGURE 1.11 *Battle of Chickamauga*

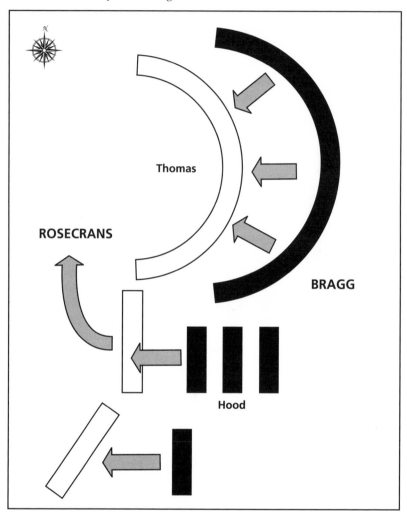

show a weakness. The cavalry would be deployed in advance of the front initially so as to maintain contact with the enemy and to determine the location of his strength. Later it would deploy on both flanks as a screening force to warn of an attacker's turning movement or envelopment. A well-posted defender could usually defeat a direct attack upon his position, even when superior numbers conducted the attack.

Interestingly, the Iraqis followed this traditional pattern in 1991. They anchored their flanks, left on the Persian Gulf and right on the

FIGURE 1.12 *Second Mannassas Campaign*

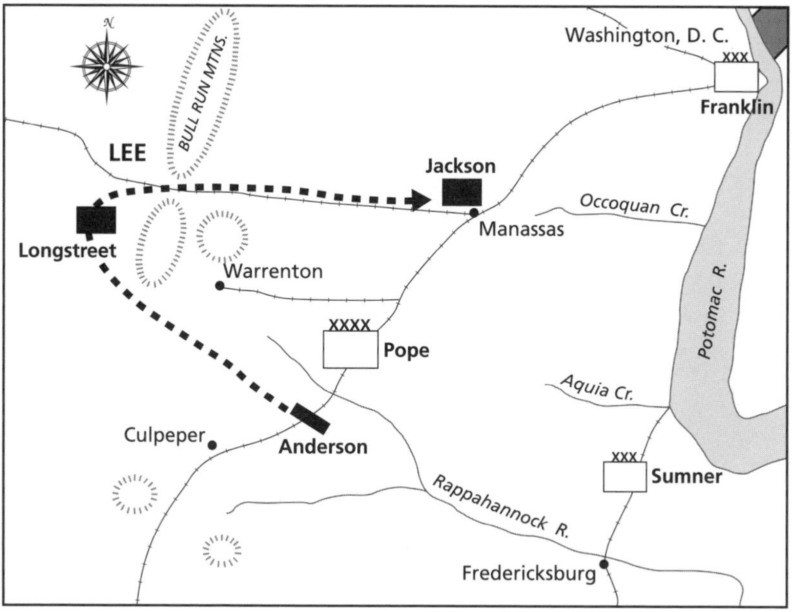

"impassable" desert. They kept strong reserves. However, their "cavalry" (air reconnaissance) was taken out of the campaign early. Their right flank proved vulnerable to both envelopment and a turning movement, because GPS allowed the U.S. forces to navigate across the desert. Additionally, the massive artillery and air bombardment weakened their positions and made movement of their reserves very difficult.

The Iraqis adapted after their 1991 defeat and adopted a different pattern during Operation Iraqi Freedom in 2003, attempting to hold only key choke points such as bridges, causeways, and urban areas. This tactic failed as well, although had the Iraqi army fought hard and had the Iraqi populace supported the regime, things could have turned out very different—as shown by the effectiveness of the ensuing insurgency.

Retrograde

There are three forms of the retrograde, all of which were used during the Civil War: the delay, the withdrawal, and the retirement.

A delay is undertaken when a force, in contact with the enemy, retreats slowly, trading space for time. The idea is to give up ground

FIGURE 1.13 *The Perryville Campaign*

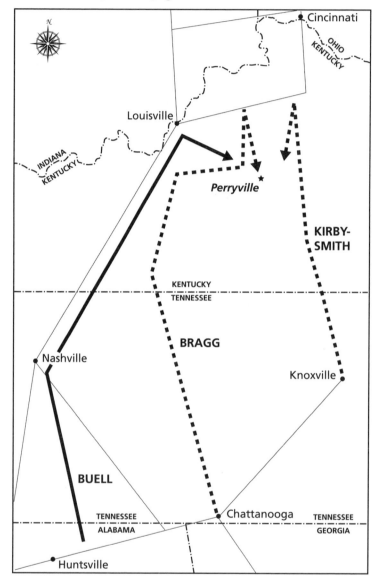

FIGURE 1.14 *Modern Example–Desert Storm*

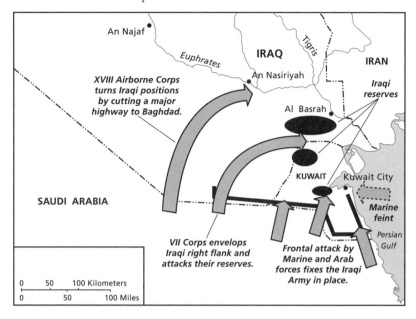

FIGURE 1.15 *Typical Defensive Positions*

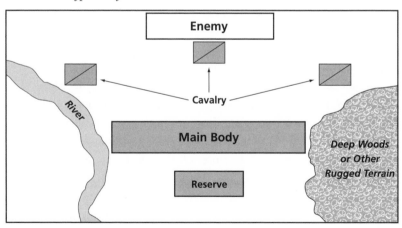

FIGURE 1.16 *Delays*

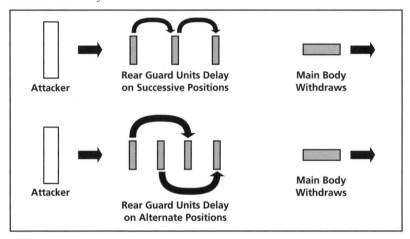

grudgingly. At likely places, the delaying force may set up an ambush, slowing down the enemy pursuit, causing casualties and a reluctance on the part of the enemy units to follow aggressively. The delaying force may even set up a regular defensive position, causing the attacker to stop, conduct a reconnaissance, and deploy for an attack, perhaps sustaining casualties and certainly losing time. Just before the attack is delivered, the defender retreats, forcing the attacker to reform his marching columns and resume his march. The toughest problems for the delaying commander are choosing the right moment to pull out of his ambush or delay position, and then disseminating that order to all of his forces. Two delaying techniques are used: delay on successive positions and delay on alternate positions. Figure 1.16 illustrates both types of delays.

During the Civil War, delay on successive positions by a designated rear guard was preferred because of the difficulty in coordinating between units occupying alternate positions. The Peninsula Campaign in 1862, shown in figure 1.17, offers an example of the Confederate Army delaying McClellan's advance until favorable conditions for an attack could be established.

A withdrawal differs from a delay in that the withdrawing force attempts to break contact with the enemy and to retreat to a new position unmolested. Because it is vulnerable to a quick attack, particularly at the moment it starts moving, the withdrawing army may try to hide its move by starting at night or in bad weather or by launching a diversionary attack to cover the movement of the main body.

FIGURE 1.17 *Peninsula Campaign*

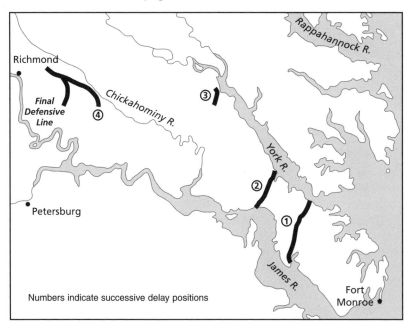

Numbers indicate successive delay positions

In 1862, after the Battle of Shiloh, General P. G. T. Beauregard withdrew his Confederate Army from Corinth, Mississippi, to Tupelo, Mississippi, as soon as Major General Henry Halleck's overwhelming force drew into position in front of Corinth (figure 1.18). The Confederate Army successfully broke contact with the assistance of such deceptive tactics as cheering, heavy artillery fire, aggressive movements, and numerous train arrivals. These fooled Halleck into thinking that Beauregard was much stronger than he was and that he was about to attack. The Confederate Army moved 50 miles south, effectively ending the campaign. Halleck decided not to pursue because of his supply difficulties, his desire to consolidate his gains, and his aspiration to seize territory—particularly the cities of Memphis and Chattanooga.

A retirement is the retrograde movement of a force not in contact with the enemy. The force may be retreating from an exposed position, where it could be cut off, or it may retire from a post that the commander deems less important than another. Figure 1.19 shows an example of a retirement due to being in an exposed location. Confederate General Albert Sidney Johnston retired from a forward position at Bowling Green,

FIGURE 1.18 *Beauregard Withdraws*

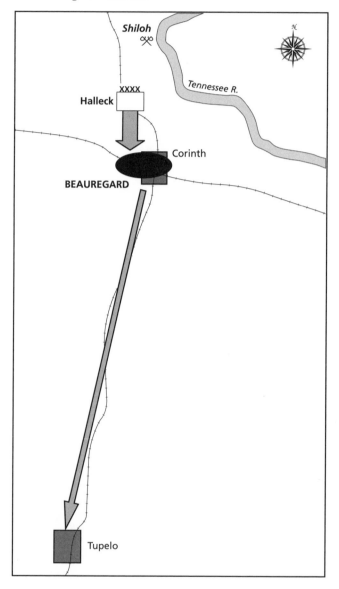

FIGURE 1.19 *Johnston Retires*

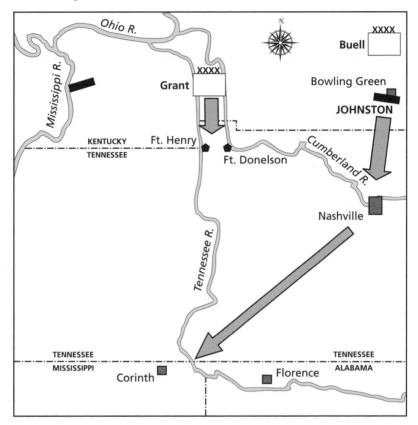

Kentucky, in February 1862. Although Johnston's army at Bowling Green was not yet in contact with opposing Union forces under General Buell, Union Brigadier General Ulysses S. Grant's seizure of Fort Henry 100 miles to the west on the Tennessee River in essence turned his position. The loss of Fort Henry meant that Union gunboats and river steamers could land and supply large bodies of troops anywhere along the Tennessee as far south as Florence, Alabama. Johnston sent reinforcements to try to hold Fort Donelson on the Cumberland River, downstream of Nashville, Tennessee, and retired with the rest of his forces to Nashville. When Donelson fell, he further retired all the way to Corinth.

Giving up ground during the Civil War without losing soldiers, wagons, artillery, supplies, and wounded men was very difficult. Almost inevitably someone would not get the word promptly or the enemy would interfere with the operation.

SUMMARY

Although the details of execution may differ, the classic forms of the offensive, defensive, and retrograde are as valid today as they were 140 years ago. A complete discussion of these operations in their modern context—with examples from the Civil War—may be found in the U.S. Army's Field Manual 100-5, *Operations*, available to the public through Brassey's Publishing. Gilham's *Manual of Instruction for the Volunteers and Militia of the United States*—published in 1861 by one of Lieutenant General Jackson's fellow professors at the Virginia Military Institute—offers an entire chapter on "Battles" in a Civil War context.[2]

END-OF-CHAPTER NOTES

1. T. R. Phillips, *Roots of Strategy* (Harrisburg, Pennsylvania: The Military Service Publishing Company, 1955), 26.

2. Major William Gilham, *Manual of Instruction for the Volunteers and Militia of the United States* (Philadelphia: Cushings & Bailey of Baltimore, MD, 1861), Article XV.

CHAPTER 2

Combat Functions

T he 1993 version of U.S. Army Field Manual 100-5, *Operations*, lists combat functions: intelligence, maneuver, fire support, air defense, mobility and survivability, logistics, and battle command. With the obvious exception of air defense, these functions were also relevant in the Civil War and are the subject of this chapter.

Types of maneuvers and fire support—the artillery—were extensively discussed in chapter 1. Survivability in the Civil War meant the use of fortifications and entrenchments, also discussed briefly in chapter 1. Battle command at the operational level is the subject of this entire book, but because the commander's staff and communications both are part of battle command, communications and the staff (and the functions of staff members) are discussed in this chapter on combat functions, along with intelligence, mobility, and logistics.

INTELLIGENCE

The Civil War commander gathered information about his enemy via six methods: direct observation; cavalry reconnaissance; reports from "scouts" (we might also call them spies); interrogation of civilians, deserters, and prisoners; intercepted signals and dispatches; and newspapers published in enemy territory. Although some maps were available— and, for instance, Sherman had been assigned in northern Georgia as a young officer and was very familiar with the area—often terrain intelligence was needed as well. Various organizations gathered information with varying levels of success, but there was no equivalent to a modern intelligence staff officer who could integrate these sources into a coherent picture. The commander was his own intelligence officer.[1]

A member of the commander's staff, the provost marshal—the chief of the military police—controlled two of the sources: reports from spies and the interrogation of civilians, deserters, and prisoners. Spies were routinely used by both sides, although their reports varied widely in reliability. Soldiers deserted from both armies, but Confederate deserters gained more attention because their homes usually lay in Northern-occupied territory and they were therefore apprehended by the other side more often. Prisoners were gathered in the innumerable small skirmishes that preceded any battle, as well as during the major battles themselves. Because there was no language barrier, such sources were extensively employed and proved to be very useful.* Civilians often voluntarily brought in information, although it was often incorrect or misleading due to their inexperience. Spies brought information about the terrain and even, in a few cases, the plans of the enemy commander. It was not unusual for a commander to be well informed of the exact locations and strengths of his opponent's major units and even his opponent's intentions.

Direct observation included the observations of the commander and his subordinates as well as those of the various signal stations—such as those shown in photos 2.1 and 2.2—which had a secondary mission of

---

* For example, consider this report from *38 OR 4:71*, containing the interrogation notes from a Confederate prisoner captured by Hooker's XX Corps, Army of the Cumberland, during the opening moves of the campaign:

Statement of Albert Smith, prisoner of war.

I was captured late this evening about half a mile from Buzzard Roost Gap, near the rail-road. I belong to the Thirty-sixth Alabama Infantry, Clayton's brigade, Stewart's division. There are about 42,000 infantry about Dalton, unless re-enforced since last night. Of these there are 11,000 men posted in Buzzard Gap, comprising Stewart's and Breckinridge's old divisions, commanded, I think, by Bate. Hindman's and Stevenson's divisions, numbering about 10,000, are stationed about five miles and a half north of Dalton, lying between the East Tennessee railroad and the mountain. Cleburne's division, about 6,000 strong, is on Hindman's right, between him and the railroad. The position of the three latter divisions is strongly intrenched.

There is a good deal of artillery, none of it heavier than 10-pounder caliber. The horses are not in good condition, and would not stand a long march. The rebels were working all last night fortifying Buzzard Roost Gap, and have masked batteries at points all along through it. The low ground has been all overflowed by dams, so that you can't travel the road, except close up to the hill. The dams are covered over with brush to conceal them. Forrest was reported last night to be within ten hours' ride of Resaca. Johnston is reported to have said that he wished the Federals would go to his (rebel) left; that he would rather have them attempt a flank there than on his right. The army is full of confidence in Johnston and of whipping the United States forces, and intend to make a desperate struggle.

Taken before me this 8th day of May, 1864.

H. M. DUFFIELD,
Lieutenant and Assistant Provost-Marshal-General.

This prisoner's data was generally correct—even down to the details!

PHOTO 2.1 *A Union signal tower near New Market, Virginia. Both sides used these to pass messages and to observe and report military movements. Flag (wig-wag) signals were used in daylight and torches at night.* PHOTO ARC 524719, NATIONAL ARCHIVES

PHOTO 2.2 *A Union tripod signal at Pulpit Rock on Lookout Mountain.* PHOTO LC-B811-3661B, LIBRARY OF CONGRESS

observing and reporting on enemy activities. Observation balloons were first used for warfare during the Civil War, but were not used in the Western Theater.

The commander would normally order his cavalry to maintain contact with the enemy through vigorous patrolling. The chief of cavalry for the army would coordinate the patrols and report results to the commander. Such reconnaissance was valuable, because the cavalry brought in information about the terrain, quizzed civilians, and sometimes captured enemy soldiers who could be interrogated. Often, however, the cavalry's information primarily concerned the positions and actions of the opposing cavalry! Confederate cavalry was usually more efficient at information gathering.

Intercepted signals, telegrams, dispatches, and letters were often sources of relevant information. Although truly important material was usually enciphered, letters home and routine letters between headquarters often gave important details about the enemy. Both sides used signal flags, but Union signalers broke the Confederate codes, giving the Union a tactical advantage.[2]

Newspapers often provided useful information to the enemy. They were routinely traded between the opposing soldiers in the picket—security outpost—lines, so, for instance, an *Atlanta Intelligencer* article discussing the Confederate Army might be in Sherman's hands in two or three days. Both sides suffered from the tendency of newsmen to write about the army's capabilities and plans. Sherman's opinion was this:

Newspaper correspondents with an army, as a rule, are mischievous. They are the world's gossips, pick up and retail the camp scandal, and gradually drift to the headquarters of some general, who finds it easier to make a reputation at home than with his own corps or division. They are also tempted to prophesy events and state facts which, to an enemy, reveal a purpose in time to guard against it.[3]

There are those who believe that not much has changed about newspaper correspondents in the last 140 years!

Both sides made maps during the war. A compilation of these is available in the *Atlas to the Official Records of the Union and Confederate Armies* (U.S. War Dept., 1889–95). The maps used for planning purposes were often inaccurate or out of date, causing confusion among the forces trying to follow them. Photo 2.3 shows an excellent map issued to Union forces on 6 May 1864.

In addition, Sherman employed new and unique sources of intelligence: the census tables of 1860 and a compilation of the tax records of Georgia.[4] These sources allowed him to gauge how much food for men and animals he could seize from the civilians in northern Georgia and therefore how much he could reduce the size of his supply train.

Intelligence, one of the most important and manpower-intensive functions of modern warfare, was carried out in a fragmented fashion in the Civil War. In some ways, however, the personal involvement of the commander in analyzing and integrating the information received

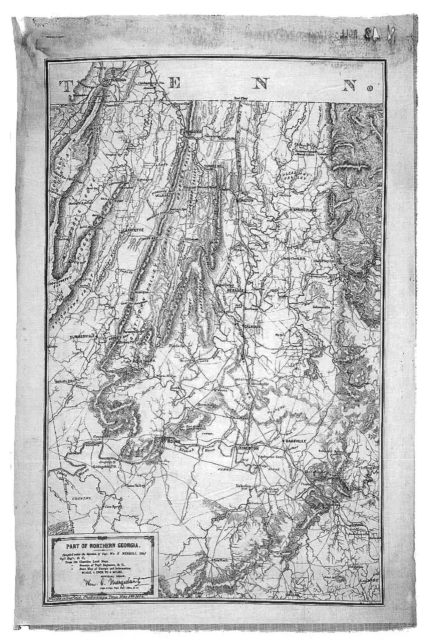

PHOTO 2.3 *This map of Northern Georgia, prepared by Union topographers and printed on May 6th, 1864, clearly shows the area covered by the initial phases of the campaign.* MAP ARC 305659, NATIONAL ARCHIVES

made up for its fragmented collection. The competent commander was well informed about his enemy's capabilities and often about his intentions as well.

MOBILITY

Almost all types of operations involve movement to some extent. An army corps, the basic unit of movement during the Civil War, would usually move on its own road or several adjacent roads. Marching rates varied greatly according to circumstances. For instance, a unit advancing toward the enemy could be expected to move slowly and with caution to prevent ambush, yet a unit that was not in danger of contacting the enemy could move much more quickly. Large units sometimes marched over 25 miles and sometimes fewer than 8 miles per day, but the average—assuming no enemy interference—was probably 12 to 15 miles per day.[5]

Because the Confederate armies generally had fewer provisions, they carried less, individually and collectively, and often could move farther and faster in a day's march. A corps column on a single road without its wagon trains could occupy 5 to 10 miles of road and up to 15 miles if its wagon trains were included.

All types of units moved on roads—infantry and cavalry—because movement was quicker and easier and the units would not become separated or disorganized. Roads were a necessity for the movement of artillery and supply wagons: the roads had to be repaired and maintained by engineers. Sometimes dedicated engineer troops were available, but often infantry regiments were detailed to engineering tasks (see photo 1.1). If a river had to be crossed, existing bridges, ferries, and fords were used when available otherwise a pontoon bridge (tethered boats carrying a roadway as illustrated in photo 1.4) had to be built. Pontoon trains (wagons carrying the boats and lumber for the roadway) were available but moved slowly and took time to install.

Often during the war railroads were used to move troops long distances relatively quickly, but these movements usually were behind friendly lines and not vulnerable to enemy action. For instance, in September 1863 two divisions of Longstreet's Corps of the Confederate Army of Northern Virginia were moved from north of Richmond, Virginia, to south of Chattanooga, Tennessee (925 miles by rail), in just a few days. The movement gave General Bragg the additional strength he needed to defeat Major General Rosecrans at Chickamauga.

LOGISTICS

The most important and least understood staff area, both during the Civil War and now, is logistics. The ability to supply soldiers and their horses and mules determined which operations could be attempted and when they were feasible. Options that appeared promising on a map in Washington or in Richmond became totally unrealistic on the ground, because the logistics support available, such as supplies or infrastructure (roads and railroads), failed to meet requirements.

Requirements

The army needed four different types of supplies: food for men, horses, and mules (including water in areas that had little); ammunition; clothing and equipment; and medical supplies. Additionally, each army had to transport a certain amount of accompanying baggage in addition to these consumable supplies.[6]

According to Sherman, each soldier required three pounds of food per day. If beef cattle accompanied the soldiers, to be slaughtered when

PHOTO 2.4 *A Union commissary near Rocky Face Ridge, supporting Sherman's advance.* PHOTO ARC 524679, NATIONAL ARCHIVES

needed, the food allowance could be cut in half, but the cattle depleted the forage used by the army's horses and mules. Each soldier usually started a movement with three days of food, precooked, in his haversack. Sherman also planned to carry food for about 25 percent more men than the effective strength of the army to feed noncombatants such as teamsters.[7] Photo 2.4 shows a Union commissary—an issue point for food—near Rocky Face Ridge at the start of the campaign.

A Civil War army had large numbers of horses and mules, horses for the cavalry and the artillery, and mules for the supply wagons. A typical army might have an animal for every three men, and sometimes even one for every two men.[8] Each horse required about 26 pounds of food per day. Almost half of this (12 pounds) was carried in wagons, and the rest was grass foraged by the horses from the roadsides and fields. The best food for animals—other than grass and hay foraged from the field—was oats, with some corn or carrots if available.[9] Mules required 23 to 24 pounds of food daily, of which 9 to 10 was carried in their wagon.[10, 11]

Each soldier carried 40 to 60 rounds of ammunition apiece into battle; more ammunition was carried by wagons, often accompanying the regiment, at the rate of one wagonload per 200 men.[12, 13] During a major battle the average infantryman might fire more than 40 rounds.[14] Artillery batteries usually carried most of their ammunition in accompanying "limber boxes" and "caissons," but the baggage train usually carried several additional wagonloads for each battery.[15]

Ambulances were provided at a rate of one wagon per regiment, about two per thousand men. The regimental surgeon and his orderlies would ride the ambulance, which usually accompanied the regiment on the march.[16] Often the regimental band members (when there was a band) would double as surgeon's orderlies, carrying the wounded back for treatment. Medical evacuation from the army—casualties or the sick—to hospitals in the rear was usually accomplished by the wagons and railroad cars that brought supplies and reinforcements to the army, although there were some dedicated hospital railroad cars as well. Such evacuation was slow and painful, with many dying along the way and even more dying in the hospital due to the lack of proper medical care.

Daily resupply requirements, not including supplies and repair parts needed during or after a battle, were just those of food, water, and forage. Six mules per wagon, 20 horses per artillery piece, 3 artillery pieces

PHOTO 2.5 *An unhitched wagon of the Union army. On a good road, drawn by 6 mules, this wagon could carry up to 3,000 pounds of supplies 15 miles a day.* PHOTO ARC 525171, NATIONAL ARCHIVES

per thousand men, and about 70 horses per thousand men as cavalry and officer mounts were average in the Western Theater during the Civil War, yielding about one animal for every three men. This is about 13 pounds of resupply per effective man per day—three for the man, one for noncombatants, and nine for the man's pro rata share of an animal. When foraging and driving beef cattle reduce hauling requirements, the resupply needs could be as low as six pounds per man per day.

Armies have two major transportation requirements: supplies and equipment that the army must carry along and items that the army consumes. To carry items other than food, there were about 13 wagons per thousand men.[17] Sherman additionally required 20 days' supply of food to be carried by the wagon trains.[18] Typically, a Civil War army would have about 40 wagons per thousand men to carry its standard load (including food) and to bring forward daily resupply from the railroad or other base. At times the total was more than 50 wagons per thousand men.[19] These wagon trains—the word "trains" survives in present military usage—were often organized by corps and kept well to the rear of any fighting.

Separated from their trains, the men could subsist for about three or four days and fight one major engagement with what they carried on their backs. After that, the men had to have fresh supplies.

Supply from the Countryside—Foraging

During his march across Georgia from Atlanta to Savannah (after the campaign under present study), Sherman was able to move twelve to fifteen miles per day, foraging for his supplies. However, "Sherman's March to the Sea" faced no real opposition (and therefore needed little ammunition), and it was harvest season in Georgia, with bountiful supplies available in the countryside.[20] A stationary or slowly moving army would not be able to count on foraging and would have to be resupplied at nearly the full rate.[21] The relatively low population density in the South prior to the Civil War (as compared with Europe or the northeastern United States, for instance) meant that there was only a limited amount of food available to be foraged in any area. During most of the Civil War, foraging could only supplement and not replace supplies from the rear.

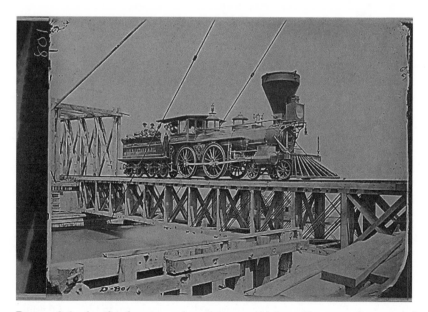

PHOTO 2.6 *A railroad engine such as this one could draw 20 wagons (boxcars) each loaded with 10 tons, for a total of 200 tons of supply.* PHOTO ARC 525206, NATIONAL ARCHIVES

FIGURE 2.1 *Extra Wagons Needed for Supply Away from a Railroad*

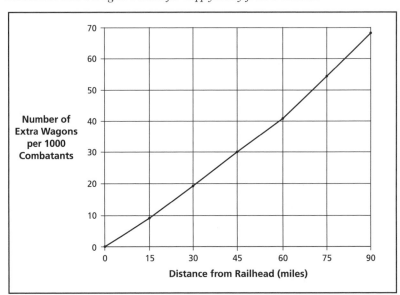

Wagons

Wagons, drawn by six mules (sometimes four mules in the Confederate Army), could haul 2,000 to 3,000 pounds over dirt roads at a rate of 2.5 miles per hour for six to eight hours a day.[22, 23, 24, 25] The ability of wagons to support an army away from a base or railroad was limited by the rate of march—15 to 20 miles per day—and by the need to carry oats or other food for the mules, 54 to 60 pounds per day, assuming that they could forage as well. Photo 2.5 shows a typical baggage wagon. Figure 2.1 gives some idea of the increasing number of wagons needed as the one-way distance from the railhead increased.

Figure 2.1 optimistically assumes that each wagon carries 3,000 pounds initially and can cover 15 miles a day. As the figure shows, greater distances would require proportionally more wagons as diminishing returns set in.

Railroads

Railroads carried much more tonnage than wagons. A typical boxcar could carry up to 10 tons and a locomotive such as that shown in photo 2.6 could draw as many as 20 cars, or 60 days' supply for 1,000 men.[26] Railroads made the assembly and support of large armies feasible in the Civil War but limited their mobility—armies were tied to their railroads. The railroads were vulnerable to raiders and required significant protective forces. During the Atlanta campaign, Sherman used more than 30 men per mile of track as static guards, primarily in blockhouses protecting trestles, to safeguard his railroads south of Nashville to Chattanooga.[27] He also left mobile units—infantry and cavalry—in key locations such as Decatur, Alabama, and Huntsville, Alabama, and directed raids from Memphis into northern Mississippi. These raids were to keep the Confederates on the defensive, away from his rail lines.

Riverboats

In many ways, riverboats were even better than railroads at moving supplies. A typical riverboat like the *Chattanooga* (shown in photo 2.7) might carry more than a train, and was less vulnerable to enemy action. However, riverboats were constrained by the water level in the river—often needing six or seven feet of water depth. More importantly, they were limited to resupplying bases on the riverbanks, so an army dependent on river transportation was tied to the river itself and the vagaries of its water levels.

Summary

The supply and transportation of a field army were (and are still) highly complex processes that often broke down. Many grandiose plans failed because of the inability of wagon transport moving on unimproved roads to support a marching army.

COMMUNICATIONS

Civil War commanders used five modes of communication with their superiors and subordinates: personal conversation, couriers, telegraph, letters, and signal flags.

Of these, the most important was the first: personal conversation. A commander would ride to his subordinates' positions to see their situations in person and to issue detailed instructions, or else he would call in his subordinates for a council of war. Personal visits were the best way to ensure that the subordinates understood his orders, but unfortunately they took the commander away from his command post, and messages from superiors or other subordinates reached him late or not at all.

Couriers, bearing either written or verbal instructions, were the next best method. Young staff officers, familiar with the commander's thoughts, could be sent on horseback or on foot to the subordinate. These young officers could not only deliver a message, but they could also amplify it by answering questions based on their understanding of the situation and the commander's intent. As representatives of the commanding general, they wielded his authority, but their relatively low rank sometimes meant delay when subordinate generals disagreed with the guidance they offered. As the subordinate generals also knew, sometimes these couriers could misquote a verbal message, misread the commander's intent, or misunderstand the situation on the ground. Frequently they also got lost or captured and never delivered the message at all!

The telegraph usually was used for strategic and operational communications—the capital to the field or between regional headquarters—and, by the Union, from headquarters on one wing of the army to another.[28]

Commanders occasionally used letters to convey lengthy instructions and diagrams. Couriers usually carried these letters, but sometimes important messages were entrusted to the mail. (See, for instance, U.S. Department of War, *War of the Rebellion: A Compilation of the Official Records of the Union and Confederate Armies*, Washington, D.C.: U.S. Government Printing Office, 1890–1901, Volume 32, Part 3, 261. Hereafter *Official Records* references will be in shorthand, 32 *OR* 3:261. The letter describes Sherman's concern that a package containing projected lines of operation for all Union armies, delivered by mail, had been opened by an unauthorized person.)

Commanders on both sides used signal flag stations extensively. These stations were sited on commanding terrain or on platforms built for the purpose. Signalers, several to each station, would encode messages and send them to other stations within eyesight. Signalers also observed the enemy and reported on any significant activities that they saw. Signal stations were difficult to establish and much less effective in bad weather or at night—when torches were used instead of flags—but they were easier to lay out than field telegraph wire. The enemy could often see their signals as well and sometimes broke the rather simple codes used, either by logic or by capturing the codebook. The Union Army was able to read Confederate signals during the Atlanta campaign, but because much of the traffic was information about what they could see the Union Army doing, this gave them only a small advantage.

The lack of timely and clear communications was a major factor in the slowness with which battles developed and the major cause of uncertainty in commanders. Messages were often misleading, being composed hastily and based on information that was hours old. There were few vantage points that allowed the commander to see or communicate with more than a fraction of the battlefield, so he had to give general instructions and hope that his subordinates could understand his intent and execute their part of the overall plan. Even now, delayed and incomplete communications hamper military operations.

BATTLE COMMAND—STAFF

The commander had a small staff in the field with him, organized quite differently from those of modern military units. Civil War staffs were made up primarily of specialists concerned with narrow areas of responsibility, unlike the broad powers residing in a modern coordinating staff.* A typical field army headquarters ranged from 200 to 1,000 men—a relatively small number.

The closest approximation to the modern chief of staff was the adjutant general, who, with his assistants, handled official correspondence of

---

* See, for instance, 38 OR 4:23. A large staff coordinated the entire theater of war—the Military Division of the Mississippi—also under Sherman's command, located in Nashville. From that source:

SPECIAL FIELD ORDERS, }   HDQRS. MIL. DIV. OF THE MISS.,

Numbers 1.}   Chattanooga, Tenn., May 3, 1864.

The following officers will compose the staff of the general commanding in the field, and will be obeyed and respected accordingly:

Personal staff: Major J. C. McCoy, aide-de-camp; Captain L. M. Dayton, aide-de-camp; Captain J. C. Audenried, aide-de-camp.

General staff: chief of artillery, Brigadier General W. F. Barry, U.S. Volunteers; chief engineer, Captain O. M. Poe, U.S. Engineers; chief quartermaster, Colonel L. C. Easton, U.S. Army; chief commissary, Colonel A. Beckwith, U.S. Army; chief of ordnance, Captain Thomas G. Baylor, U.S. Army; medical inspector, Surg. E. D. Kittoe, U.S. Volunteers; inspectors-general, Brigadier General J. M. Corse, U.S. Volunteers, Lieutenant Colonel Charles Ewing, Captain, Thirteenth U.S. Infantry, Lieutenant Colonel Willard Warner, Seventy-sixth Ohio Volunteers.

Reports and applications requiring immediate action will be addressed by generals commanding separate armies directly to the commander-in-chief; by subordinates to Capt. L. M. Dayton, aide-de-camp. All current business will, as heretofore, be addressed to Lieut. Col. R. M. Sawyer, assistant adjutant-general of the division headquarters, Nashville, Tenn.

W. T. SHERMAN
Major General, Commanding

PHOTO 2.7 *The steamer* Chattanooga, *built by Union troops and docked at the railhead at Bridgeport, Alabama, carried several hundred tons each trip up the Tennessee River to Chattanooga, supplying Sherman's army.* PHOTO ARC 530459, NATIONAL ARCHIVES

all types for the commander. The quartermaster supervised all types of supplies except food and ordnance; he usually controlled the movement of the baggage trains. The commissary, a commissioned officer, handled food procurement and, like the quartermaster, on many questions answered directly to his superiors in the national capital rather than to the army commander. A chief of ordnance supervised weapons and ammunition procurement and maintenance. Inspectors general examined troop units and accounts and sometimes were given special assignments. As already mentioned, the provost marshal was the military policeman, issuing passes to civilians and military personnel and detaining prisoners. Other specialized officers on many staffs included the chaplain, the engineer, the signal officer, the medical inspector, and the judge advocate (legal officer). The chief of artillery and the chief of cavalry would oversee their respective branches and advise the commander on their use; they also sometimes commanded elements of their branch in battle. Additionally, the commander would have a number of aides-de-camp and mounted orderlies to courier messages.[29] The idea of a modern coordinating staff, with a chief of staff, a personnel officer, an intelligence officer, an operations officer, a logistics officer, and a communications officer, had not yet been discussed in military circles, much less adopted. In the Civil War, members of the staff acted as individual advisors, not as a coordinated body. Coordination was achieved only via the commander.

END-OF-CHAPTER NOTES

1. Jay Luvaas, "'One or Two Good Spies,' Sherman's Use of Intelligence," 4th U.S. Army War College International Conference on Intelligence and Strategy, Carlisle Barracks, Pennsylvania, 9–11 May 1989.

2. See, for instance, *Memoirs of General William T. Sherman* (New York: Da Capo Press, Inc., 1984), Volume II, 54 (hereafter referred to as "Sherman's Memoirs").

3. Sherman's Memoirs, Vol. II, 408.

4. Sherman's Memoirs, Vol. II, 31.

5. Edward Hagerman, *The American Civil War and the Origins of Modern Warfare* (Bloomington, Indiana: Indiana University Press, 1992), 286.

6. Hagerman, 77.

7. Sherman's Memoirs, Vol. II, 389.

8. Hagerman, 279.

9. Robert M. Thomas, *The (Old) Farmer's Almanack* (Boston: Brewer & Tileston, 1864), 37.

10. Hagerman, 44.

11. John G. Moore, "Mobility and Strategy in the Civil War," *Military Affairs* 24 (1960), 68.

12. Hagerman, 77.

13. U.S. Department of War, *War of the Rebellion: A Compilation of the Official Records of the Union and Confederate Armies* (Washington, D.C.: U.S. Government Printing Office, 1890–1901), Volume 38, Part 4, 159. Hereafter Official Records references will be in shorthand, 38 *OR* 4:159.

14. Paddy Griffith, *Battle Tactics of the Civil War* (New Haven, Connecticut: Yale University Press, 1989), 85.

15. Paddy Griffith, *Battle in the Civil War* (Camberley, England: Fieldbooks, 1986), 26.

16. 38 *OR* 4:159

17. Hagerman, 77.

18. 32 *OR* 3:479.

19. Hagerman, 279.

20. Hagerman, 286.

21. Moore, 69.

22. Hagerman, 45.

23. Sherman's Memoirs, Vol. II, 389.

24. Griffith, *Battle in the Civil War*, 9.

25. Moore, 71.

26. Sherman's Memoirs, Vol. II, 399.

27. 32 *OR* 3:290–1.

28. Hagerman, 81–7.

29. 38 *OR* 4:23.

CHAPTER 3

Decisions, Campaigns, and Styles of Warfare

This chapter gives background information on military decision making, the operational level of war (campaign planning and styles of warfare), and specific details applicable to the Civil War. The first section outlines briefly two key ideas from the acknowledged master theorists Clausewitz and Sun Tzu. The second section discusses military decisions, and the third covers some of the tenets of campaign planning from the modern perspective. The final section discusses several theoretical styles of warfare using modern era examples.

CONSIDERATION OF THE CLASSICS

Soldiers and other experts in military affairs honor two classic works above all others: Carl von Clausewitz's *On War* and Sun Tzu's *Art of War*. Although neither book was well known (if at all) by the generals fighting the Civil War, both are now considered classics because they offer insight into the problems of a general. Many theorists try to put them into opposition to each other—see, for instance, the "Styles of Warfare" section later in this chapter on attrition versus maneuver—but in essence these two very different people covered many of the same ideas and did so in such clear, complete manners that their works are still referred to by current theorists. Selective quotes are provided from each to illustrate examples of some of their most important insights.

Clausewitz on Friction

Everything in war is very simple, but the simplest thing is difficult. The difficulties accumulate and end by producing a kind of friction that is inconceivable unless one has experienced war. . . . Countless minor incidents—the kind you can never really foresee—combine to lower the general level of performance, so that one always falls far short of the intended goal. . . . A battalion is made up of individuals, the least important of whom may chance to delay things or somehow make them go wrong. The dangers inseparable from war and the physical exertions war demands can aggravate the problem to such an extent that they must be ranked among its principal causes. . . . Action in war is like movement in a resistive element. Just as the simplest and most natural of movements, walking, cannot easily be performed in water, so in war it is difficult for normal efforts to achieve even modest results.[1]

Not only does this account for the emphasis on simplicity often seen—the KISS (for Keep It Simple, Stupid) principle is enshrined in Army lore—but it also explains why plans always call for less effort or ability (movement speed, firing rates, accuracy, transport capacity, and so on) than one would expect from theory.

Sun Tzu on Deception

Sun Tzu said: . . . Warfare is the Way (Tao) of deception. Thus, although [you are] capable, display incapability to them. When committed to employing your forces, feign inactivity.[2] . . . Thus the army is established by deceit, moves for advantage, and changes through segmenting and reuniting. . . . It is as difficult to know as the darkness; in movement it is like thunder.[3] . . . [The general] alters his management of affairs and changes his strategies to keep other people from recognizing them. He shifts his positions and travels indirect routes to keep other people from being able to anticipate him.[4]

Sun Tzu, a legendary Chinese soldier, understood the advantage of keeping the enemy unsure of your intentions. If the enemy has to prepare for many possibilities, he cannot prepare thoroughly for any of them. One of the principles of war, surprise, is made possible primarily by deceiving the enemy.

The implementation of the commander's decision should include means of deception and due consideration of the effects of friction; if the staff doesn't take these key ideas into account while they plan, the odds are that they will not succeed.

MILITARY DECISIONS

The principal variable affecting how a military decision is made is the time that is available to make the decision, formulate a plan, and then disseminate that plan—including leaving adequate time for subordinates to make their own plans and rehearse their actions. This time can vary from literally a split second in the case of a soldier deciding whether to engage a target or a patrol leader reacting to an ambush, to months or even years in the case of a theater combatant commander directed to prepare an operations plan for a specified contingency. In the latter case, approval from the national capital is usually required, and it is rarely forthcoming in a timely manner.

In the first case, when instant reaction is needed, there is little or no deliberation. Soldiers react as they have been trained and as they have rehearsed. The decisions made and plans executed are those that were anticipated and hopefully trained for prior to the event.

If events occur that allow more time before a decision must be made, a military decision-making process (abbreviated MDMP) emerges. In the modern U.S. military, this process follows the outline given earlier for an estimate of the situation:

1. Analyze the mission.
2. Examine the current situation: enemy, friendly, and neutral factors that could affect mission accomplishment.
3. Develop courses of action that could accomplish the mission given the current situation.
4. Analyze each course of action to determine its advantages and disadvantages.
5. Compare the courses of action with each other and against the desired outcome.
6. Make a decision.

The depth of this estimate and the planning accompanying it vary greatly depending on the time available and the professionalism of the staff and commander. If five minutes are available, a mission analysis and the cursory consideration of perhaps two courses of action may be all that can be done. If five hours are available, there is time for at least three courses of action and some detailed analysis and comparison. As the time available increases, so does the depth—but not necessarily the quality—of the planning process.

An accomplished staff can greatly enhance the quality of planning, because the staff members keep their awareness of the situation up to date, use slack time to develop and polish contingency plans, and anticipate events. They can form an excellent estimate of the situation and consider several alternatives in a very short time.* An inexperienced or inept staff, on the other hand, rarely can do any of this well and often will waste much of the time available.

The principal benefit of this planning—the ability to incorporate detailed consideration of several courses of action—is not necessarily the decision itself. It is a cliché that "no plan survives contact with the enemy." The plan is the starting point. Of equal importance is that during the analysis and comparison of the courses of action, the commander and his or her staff have rehearsed and learned. They know a lot about the terrain and other important features of the area. They have thought about several possible enemy actions. They understand time and distance factors that facilitate or hamper various operations. They have developed contingency plans to handle emerging situations. In short, they have prepared to successfully engage a thinking, independently acting enemy, and to win their campaign.

CAMPAIGN PLANNING

The textbook definition of a campaign is "a series of major operations arranged in time, space, and purpose to achieve a strategic objective."[5] Unfortunately, this definition fails to paint a meaningful picture to most people, because it deliberately omits any specifics in the interests of being all inclusive. Although purists may quibble with the details given here, generally a military campaign can be defined in terms of space, time, objective, and committed forces.

---

* The author was privileged to lead a Special Operations Task Force during part of Operation Enduring Freedom in Afghanistan in 2002. The Task Force staff was outstanding in every respect, able to conduct detailed and accurate planning for future combat operations while simultaneously reacting to urgent requirements. They kept well ahead of demand by developing and refining a "playbook" of standard courses of action while they monitored ongoing activity and anticipated both enemy reactions and friendly activities. They were an exemplary staff and they made the operation the success it was—and taught their commanding general a lot as well!

- **Committed forces:** Usually a field army or army group (fifty to several hundred thousand soldiers in the Civil War), a naval task force if applicable, and, in modern times, an air force of several hundred aircraft. In modern times all these would be under the command of a Joint Task Force commander or a theater Combatant Commander.
- **Objective:** The city, area, or terrain feature to be captured or the end state that supports the strategic plan.
- **Time:** Variable, but usually weeks rather than hours or years.
- **Space:** Stretching over large areas, often hundreds of kilometers on a side, usually bounded by impassible or infeasible terrain such as high mountains; extensive wetlands; large rivers, lakes, seas, or oceans; or international boundaries.

A campaign plan describes how a series of major operations involving the various committed forces are to be arranged in time, space, and purpose to achieve the overall objective. It is the primary means that the overall commander—whether army in the case of the Civil War or Joint Task Force in modern terms—uses to achieve unity of effort and synchronization among his or her forces. The commander uses a campaign plan to:

- define objectives and possible end states
- describe concepts of operation and sustainment
- arrange operations and assign tasks
- organize forces and establish command relationships

Subordinates use the campaign plan as a basis for their own planning.

The estimate of the situation, created by the commander and his staff, is the foundation for the campaign plan. By following its logic, the commander and his staff are led to determine objectives (usually specific effects on enemy "centers of gravity"), to consider alternate courses of action, and finally to decide on a coordinated plan.

A campaign plan is often less detailed than the usual operations plan found at the tactical level. Typically, the plan includes significant detail about the first phase or first operation in the campaign, but subsequent operations (sequels) are only outlined. The plan may outline several alternatives (branches) for accomplishing the objectives of these subsequent operations.

A campaign employs one or more styles of warfare, depending on the capabilities of the forces available to the commander, the enemy, and the terrain. In the Civil War, a particular campaign usually employed only one distinct style of warfare.

STYLES OF WARFARE

Recently defense analysts and theoreticians have placed a lot of emphasis on "styles of warfare" pursued by different armies at different times. Often Civil War campaigns have been used to illustrate these styles. For instance, some current literature contrasts "attrition" with "maneuver" styles. Others compare "persisting" with "raiding" strategies, or "combat" versus "logistic" strategies.

Operational Modes

Archer Jones, in *The Art of War in the Western World*,[6] defined eight characteristic strategies (which I call operational modes). Table 3.1 lists these eight operational modes.

The terms used are three sets of contrasting pairs of words: offensive/defensive, combat/logistic, and persisting/raiding. Offensive refers to taking the initiative against the enemy, usually by some movement against his positions. The defensive is in some sense the opposite approach, awaiting and then attempting to defeat the enemy's initiative. A combat operational mode seeks a decision by directly engaging and trying to defeat or destroy the combat forces of the enemy, and a logistic mode avoids contact with the main force of the enemy, attacking supplies, military and civilian infrastructure or other "soft" targets. A persisting mode seeks to occupy specific areas, and a raiding mode concentrates on destroying specific objectives (combat or

TABLE 3.1 *Operational Modes*

offensive combat persisting
offensive combat raiding
offensive logistic persisting
offensive logistic raiding
defensive combat persisting
defensive combat raiding
defensive logistic persisting
defensive logistic raiding

logistic), but not on retaining their possession. In real warfare, an operational commander will mix and vary his modes depending on the situation.

Early in the American Civil War, both sides used the combat persisting mode (the Confederacy on the defensive and the Union on the offensive), but the Union soon added a logistic persisting strategy with a coastal blockade and the occupation of the Mississippi River Basin and the state of Tennessee. Both sides employed raiding as a secondary mode. Arguably, the collapse of the Confederacy was due to the loss of military and civilian morale and shortage of supplies caused by General Sherman's successful execution of the offensive logistic raiding mode against Georgia

Modern Example

The war in Vietnam illustrated many of these operational modes. The U.S. military employed an offensive combat raiding mode against the North Vietnamese in remote areas (the so-called "big unit war" or campaign). The United States and South Vietnamese employed a defensive persisting mode—both combat and logistic—in populated areas (the pacification campaign) while the air forces employed an offensive logistic raiding mode against supply lines (interdiction campaign against the Ho Chi Minh trail and roads and railroads in North Vietnam). The North Vietnamese and the Viet Cong employed an offensive combat raiding mode until Tet 68, when they switched to an offensive combat persisting mode. Although they were tactically defeated—and the Viet Cong virtually destroyed—during Tet, the long-term effect of the intense fighting was to take the United States out of the war because of Tet's effect on civilian morale in the United States. The North Vietnamese's initial renewal, after rebuilding their forces, of the offensive combat persisting mode in 1972 was also defeated,* but their final renewal of this mode in 1975 was successful, because the earlier operations—though unsuccessful on the battlefield in Vietnam—had caused the United States to withdraw its support of and its soldiers from South Vietnam.

---

* The author played a very minor role in this campaign as an infantry lieutenant in the U.S. Army.

and the Carolinas in late 1864 (his infamous "March to the Sea") and in 1865, after the end of the campaign discussed in this book.

Attrition versus Maneuver

In contrast to this rather complex idea of operational modes, the attrition versus maneuver debate prevalent in recent years addresses exclusively only attrition warfare and maneuver warfare. Attrition warfare is described as the direct clash of forces, without finesse, lasting until the superior force overwhelms the inferior. It is said to be the traditional U.S. Army style, characterized by firepower, practiced by General Grant in the Civil War, and exemplified by the theories of Clausewitz. Maneuver warfare is described as its antithesis. Maneuver warfare practitioners avoid the enemy's strengths, maneuvering against his vulnerabilities to defeat him. It is said to be the traditional German style, characterized by mobility, practiced by Lieutenant General Jackson in the Civil War, and exemplified by the writings of Sun Tzu. Note that people tying General Grant to attrition warfare forget his Vicksburg campaign, a masterpiece of maneuver ending in the siege and eventual surrender of Vicksburg.

These brief descriptions make the case for maneuver warfare almost inarguable. Unfortunately, this view is somewhat oversimplified: maneuver without threat of attrition and attrition without threat of maneuver are both wasteful and nearly pointless in any military sense. Both concepts are tightly linked. There will be maneuver as commanders seek advantage, and there will be attrition as their armies collide. Whether a battle is thought of as attrition or maneuver depends on who you are, where you are, and when you make your judgment.

Numerous campaigns—Civil War and more recent—show that the enemy is often smart or well informed enough to meet your maneuver with one of his own, precipitating the attrition neither side desires. Nevertheless, the debate over attrition versus maneuver has generated many articles and much heated discussion in military circles in recent years.[7]

Theorists debating the merits of attrition and maneuver often use campaigns and battles from the American Civil War to make their respective points. However, most Civil War generals started an offensive campaign attempting to out-maneuver their enemy and ended up with a

Attrition or Maneuver?

In the following illustration, an attacking operational commander (units shown in white) has used an operational maneuver to envelop the defending commander's left flank (units shown in gray). The latter has been outmaneuvered because there is a large force threatening his lines of communication. Not only is he undergoing attrition in his left flank unit, but also he must move some of his forces to extricate himself. He can commit his reserve to a counterattack, a maneuver that may precipitate a slugging match, or he can withdraw to the next defensive position farther back. If he is unlucky (if wind direction, his position, and/or terrain prevent him from learning of the attack in time to react properly), he may have to fight on unfavorable ground or retreat in an unexpected direction. The attacking commander's maneuver may result in an attrition-based battle under advantageous circumstances or in his opponent's loss of position due to maneuver. The outcome depends on luck, the personalities of the commanders, and on detailed circumstances.

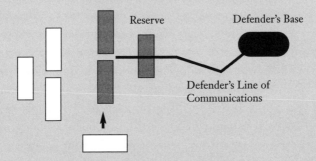

On the other hand, the subordinate defender on the left flank is faced with an unenviable tactical situation—an attrition battle on unfavorable terms. He is being enfiladed: attacking soldiers are firing along his line, but most of his soldiers cannot return fire for fear of hitting their comrades. He is taking disproportionate casualties and, without help, must retreat, surrender, or be killed.

battle characterized primarily by attrition. Their opponents had anticipated the maneuvers or had reacted in a timely manner, precipitating a
direct confrontation.

END-OF-CHAPTER NOTES

1. Carl von Clausewitz, *On War* (Michael Howard and Peter Paret, ed. and trans.;
    Princeton, New Jersey: Princeton University Press, 1976), 119–120.
2. Sun Tzu, *Art of War* (Ralph D. Sawyer, trans.; Boulder, Colorado: Westview Press,
    1994), 168.
3. Sun Tzu, 198.
4. Sun Tzu, 222.
5. Joint Pub 5-0, *Doctrine for Planning Joint Operations* (Washington, D.C.: Department
    of Defense, 1995), II–18.
6. Archer Jones, *The Art of War in the Western World* (New York: Oxford University
    Press, 1987).
7. See, for instance, Richard D. Hooker, Jr. (ed.), *Maneuver Warfare: An Anthology*
    (Novato, California: Presidio Press, 1993) for both sides of the issue, or Robert R.
    Leonhard, *The Art of Maneuver: Maneuver-Warfare Theory and AirLand Battle*
    (Novato, California: Presidio Press, 1991) for a maneuver advocate's point of view.

CHAPTER 4

Setting the Stage—
May 1864

BRIEF SUMMARY OF THE SITUATION

By the time Major General William Tecumseh "Cump" Sherman (photo 4.1) was making his final decisions about the forthcoming campaign, three years of war had already passed. War was being waged in three land theaters: the Eastern Theater in northern Virginia and along the Atlantic coast; the Western Theater in Tennessee, Mississippi, Alabama, and Georgia; and the Trans-Mississippi, west of the Mississippi River.

In the East, there was stalemate. Union gains had been slight—small portions of northern and eastern Virginia, almost all of West Virginia (a portion of Virginia that rejoined the Union as a separate state in 1863), and minor enclaves along the coasts—at the cost of horrendous casualties on both sides. Lieutenant General Grant had been called east to take charge of all Union Army forces, but in particular to supervise operations in the Eastern Theater of the war. In contrast, both sides had assigned the Trans-Mississippi sector a low priority and had expended little effort there, although the Union had made significant gains and the Confederacy was on the defensive.

In Sherman's Western Theater, east of the Mississippi and west of the Appalachian Mountains, the Confederacy was in serious trouble. The Union had totally occupied Kentucky, a border state that had been partially occupied by each side in 1861. More importantly, the Union also held the state of Tennessee, the Mississippi River, and portions of north Alabama and Georgia. Large Union armies were posed to invade the heartland of the Confederacy, central and southern Georgia, Alabama, and Mississippi (see figure 4.1). These agricultural lands and the factories in the cities of Selma and Montgomery in Alabama and Atlanta, Columbus, Macon, and Augusta in Georgia supplied all the Confederate armies with essentials. The forthcoming campaign, delayed until the

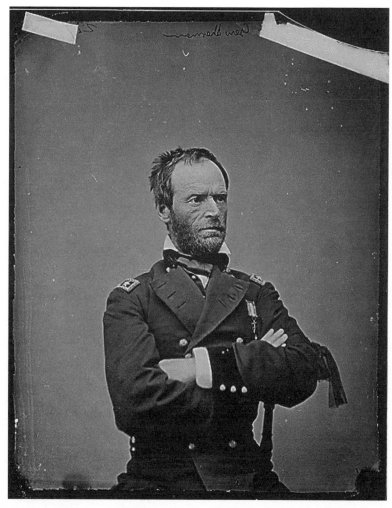

PHOTO 4.1 *Major General William Tecumseh ("Cump") Sherman, Commanding General of the Military Division of the Mississippi.* PHOTO ARC 525970, NATIONAL ARCHIVES

spring grass grew long enough to feed the horses and mules, would decide the fate of the Confederacy. The Confederate Army of Tennessee, led by General Joseph E. Johnston, stood in Sherman's way.

THE UNION POLITICAL AND COMMAND ENVIRONMENT

In early 1864, the political situation of the Union was precarious. Three years of war had resulted in only limited gains at terrible cost. The elec-

FIGURE 4.1. *The Situation in the West*

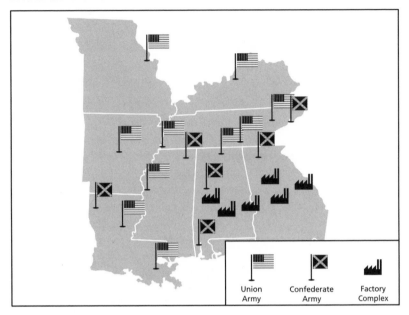

torate was to go to the polls in the fall. President Lincoln faced not only a Democratic Party openly opposed to the further prosecution of the war, but also a revolt against him personally in the ranks of the Republican Party. Without a highly visible success such as the taking of Richmond in the East or Atlanta in the West, the war-weary public might reject Lincoln and the war. In this climate, Lincoln had brought his most successful general, Grant, to Washington and put him in charge of all Union armies. Grant left the Western Theater in charge of General Sherman.

Sherman had excellent relations with his superior. Sherman had worked for Grant periodically since the Shiloh campaign, and Grant had depended on his subordinate heavily, entrusting him often with independent command. The two had had numerous face-to-face meetings about the Western Theater and had discussed possible campaign plans. Their mutual admiration and trust are exemplified by quotations from two letters. After being notified that he would be promoted to lieutenant general and placed in charge of all Union armies, Grant wrote to Sherman:

> [W]hat I want is to express my thanks to you and McPherson as the men to whom, above all others, I feel indebted for whatever I have had of success.[1]

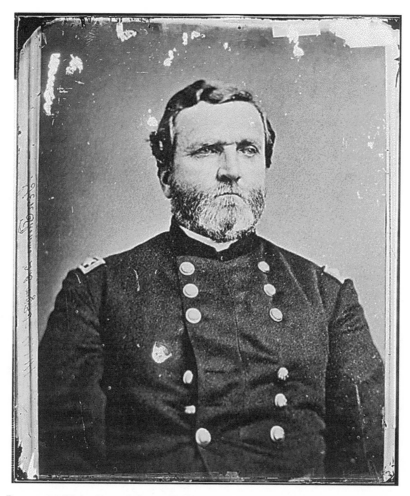

PHOTO 4.2 *Major General George H. Thomas, the "Rock of Chickamauga," Commanding General of the Army of the Cumberland.* PHOTO ARC 528908, NATIONAL ARCHIVES

Sherman replied:

> [Y]ou do General McPherson and myself too much honor. . . . I believe you are as brave, patriotic, and just as the great prototype, Washington; as unselfish, kind-hearted, and honest as a man should be, but the chief characteristic is the simple faith in success you have always manifested. . . .[2]

Sherman could hope for no better support from his superior.

PHOTO 4.3 *Major General James B. McPherson, Commanding General of the Army of the Tennessee.* PHOTO ARC 530371, NATIONAL ARCHIVES

Sherman had three army commanders working directly for him in the field: Major General George H. Thomas (photo 4.2), Major General James B. McPherson (photo 4.3), and Major General John M. Schofield (photo 4.4). Other generals ran various military operations for Sherman in Memphis, Nashville, and Cairo (Illinois), but these three army commanders were the subordinates he used to prosecute the campaign against Johnston.

Thomas had been Sherman's roommate at West Point and had had a far more distinguished military career than Sherman. Although accused by some to be afflicted with "the slows," his combat record was unblemished. As a corps commander, he had saved the Army of the Cumberland, his present command, from defeat at Stones River and from destruction

PHOTO 4.4 *Major General John M. Schofield, Commanding General of the Army of the Ohio.* PHOTO ARC 528310, NATIONAL ARCHIVES

at Chickamauga. Grant picked Sherman to command in the West over Thomas, who many thought should have had the appointment.

McPherson, commander of the Army of the Tennessee, was well thought of by all—as can be seen from Grant's letter quoted earlier. He had been Grant's chief engineer and then commanded a corps during the Vicksburg campaign. Schofield, by way of contrast, had little combat experience, having commanded in Missouri for most of the war. His command, the Army of the Ohio, little more than a corps in size, was also inexperienced.

In spite of this weakness, all of Sherman's three principal subordinates had shown ability in their assignments during the war to date. They provided him with dependable subordinate leadership.

END-OF-CHAPTER NOTES

1.   32 *OR* 3:18.
2.   32 *OR* 3:49.

Part Two
Estimate of the Situation

CHAPTER 5

Mission

ESTIMATE OF THE SITUATION

I. MISSION

II. THE SITUATION AND COURSES OF ACTION

III. ANALYSIS OF OPPOSING COURSES OF ACTION

IV. COMPARISON OF OWN COURSES OF ACTION

V. DECISION

The most important planning consideration for any general is, "What is my mission?" A mission is formally defined as "the task, together with the purpose, that clearly indicates the action to be taken and the reason for taking it."[1] That is, what is to be accomplished, and why? Usually the general's next higher headquarters gives him such instructions.

A general receiving instructions does not merely pass them along to his subordinates, but rather performs a "mission analysis" to ensure he understands everything he is being asked to do. Although a modern mission analysis can be quite complex, extending to intelligence, logistics, preliminary operations outlining, risk assessment, and allocation of planning time, the essentials are:

- Analyze the instructions received to determine specified and implied tasks
- Develop a restated mission that will be transmitted to subordinates

EXAMPLE

By way of example, the following directive was given to General Eisenhower by the Combined Chiefs of Staff, setting the stage for Operation Overlord, the invasion of continental Europe by the Allies.

Dated 18 February 1944, the letter set forth Eisenhower's mission. Key excerpts are provided here.

1. You are hereby designated as Supreme Allied Commander . . . for liberation of Europe from Germany.
2. You will enter the continent of Europe and, with the other United Nations, undertake operations aimed at the heart of Germany and the destruction of her Armed Forces. The date for entering the Continent is the month of May 1944. After adequate Channel ports have been secured, exploitation will be directed towards securing an area that will facilitate both ground and air operations against the enemy.
3. [Y]ou will be prepared at any time to take immediate advantage of favorable circumstances, such as withdrawal by the enemy on your front to affect a reentry into the Continent with such forces as you have available at the time.
4. *Command.* You are responsible to the Combined Chiefs of Staff. . . .
5. *Logistics.* In the United Kingdom, the responsibility for logistics organization, concentration, movement, and supply . . . will rest with British Service Ministries so far as British Forces are concerned. So far as United States Forces are concerned, this responsibility will rest with the United States War and Navy Departments. You will be responsible for the coordination of logistical arrangements on the Continent. You will be responsible for coordinating the requirements of British and United States forces under your command.
6. *Coordination of operations of other Forces and Agencies.* . . . [S]ea and air forces, agencies of sabotage, subversions, and propaganda acting under a variety of authorities, are now in action. You may recommend any variation in these activities.
7. *Relationship to United Nations Forces in other areas.* Responsibility will rest with the Combined Chiefs of Staff for supplying information relating to operations of the forces of the USSR. . . . The Allied Commander-in-Chief, Mediterranean Theater, will conduct operations designed to assist your operation, including the launching of an attack against the south of France. . . . You will establish contact with him and submit to the Combined Chiefs of Staff your views and recommendations regarding operations from the Mediterranean in support of your attack. . . . The Combined Chiefs of Staff will place under

your command the forces operating in southern France as soon as you are in a position to assume such command. You will submit timely recommendations compatible with this. . . .[2]

There are two types of tasks to be gleaned from the directive: specified tasks and implied tasks. Specified tasks are those specifically mentioned in the directive, such as "coordination of logistical arrangements on the Continent" in paragraph 5. Implied tasks are those that are not specifically called out but that can be reasonably inferred from the directive. For instance, a requirement to establish control of the English Channel between England and France can be inferred from the requirement to enter the continent of Europe. Table 5.1 graphically portrays the author's mission analysis based on this directive. Because preparations for Operation Overlord were actually far advanced by February 1944, there is no historical mission analysis based just on the directive itself. The priorities given are the opinion of the author.

Given the specified and implied tasks, the commander's next action is to restate the mission, in his own terms, to provide clear guidance to his staff and his subordinate commanders. Often, especially when planning time is short, this restated mission is the basis for issuing a warning order to subordinate units.

Eisenhower's mission, as restated by the author, is:

Enter Europe by May 1944 so as to seize control of ports and a safe lodgment area for ground and air forces. Protect the invasion force from air and sea incursions during and after the invasion, and build up a logistics base. From this lodgment area and logistics base, undertake operations against Germany and her armed forces. Coordinate logistics, special activities, and supporting operations conducted by CINC-Med with the Combined Chiefs of Staff. Be prepared to invade before May 1944 if enemy forces withdraw from areas accessible to our invasion forces. Be prepared to breach fortified areas and conduct river crossings as necessary.

Desired end state: The continent of Europe liberated from German control, the surrender or destruction of German armed forces, and the occupation of Germany by Allied forces.

TABLE 5.1 *Worksheet for Eisenhower's Tasks*

Task Description	Task Purpose/Source	Priority	Type*
1. Enter Europe in May 1944.	Necessary to accomplish task 2. (Paragraph 2)	2	S
2. Undertake operations against the heart of Germany and destroy her armed forces.	Liberate Europe. (Paragraphs 1 and 2)	1	S
3. Establish and maintain control of the sea in the English Channel.	Necessary to accomplish task 1. No seaborne invasion can succeed without controlling the sea approaches to the area.	5	I
4. Establish and maintain control of the air above the English Channel and the invasion force.	Necessary to accomplish task 1. No modern seaborne invasion has ever succeeded without controlling the air over the area.	6	I
5. Secure Channel ports.	Necessary to supply landing forces and build up strength to attack. (Paragraph 2)	3	S
6. Secure area to build up ground and air forces.	Provide space for forces adequate to accomplish task 2. (Paragraph 2)	4	S
7. Be prepared to use available forces immediately to invade if the enemy withdraws.	Take advantage of unexpected favorable circumstances should they arise. (Paragraph 3)	7	S
8. Coordinate logistical arrangements on the Continent.	Ensure that proper supplies support the invasion force. (Paragraph 5)	9	S
9. Coordinate the requirements of British and United States forces under your command.	Ensure proper prioritization of limited supply assets. (Paragraph 5)	8	S
10. Recommend any variation in special activities.	Ensure that special activities support rather than interfere with your campaign plan. (Paragraph 6)	12	S

continued

* Specified task (S) or implied task (I).

TABLE 5.1 *Worksheet for Eisenhower's Tasks, continued*

Task Description	Task Purpose/Source	Priority	Type*
11. Contact CINC-Med, submit views of his proposed support to the Combined Chiefs of Staff, and be prepared to assume command of forces that he commits to France.	Ensure maximum coordination and eventual unity of command in the theater. (Paragraph 7)	10	S
12. Be prepared to breach fortified positions and cross major rivers.	Necessary to accomplish tasks 1 and 2. Many fortified areas and major rivers lie on the path to the heart of Germany.	11	I

Of course, the number and details of implied missions, the prioritization of missions, and the details of the mission restatement would vary between different commanders and staffs. The restatement, as with many other "solutions" given later in the text, is just the author's opinion.

In the Civil War, generals often did not receive such detailed instructions. They also had no process of formal mission analysis, as the idea had not yet been conceived of. How they finally formulated their plans is poorly documented, if at all. However, it is possible to apply the modern process to the letters General Sherman received, as demonstrated in the following section.

SHERMAN'S MISSION

Many of the instructions that General Grant gave General Sherman were conveyed orally during their trip together from Nashville to Cincinnati during the period 18–20 March 1864.[3, 4] However, several letters and messages preserved in memoirs and in official records record the gist of the instructions. Excerpts from these appear on succeeding pages and, taken together, they form a solid basis for performing a mission analysis.

Additionally, there is a letter from Major General Sherman to Colonel Comstock of Grant's staff, dated 5 April 1864.[8] The letter refers to a marked map that is reproduced in *The Official Military Atlas of the Civil War* (Plate 135A) and also in map 5.1. The map has a blue line drawn from Tunnel Hill, Georgia (the current line of contact between General Thomas's Union Army of the Cumberland and General Johnston's Confederate Army of Tennessee), to Atlanta. The letter makes it obvious that

Grant desires to make the railroad Sherman's line of operation—the axis upon which Sherman should try to advance.*

These documents outline General Sherman's mission. Again, a modern commander and his staff would use the documents to determine the specific tasks to be accomplished and their purposes, prioritize them, and list any necessary intermediate or implied tasks. Finally, the commander normally would restate the mission for his unit in his own words.

[PRIVATE AND CONFIDENTIAL]

HEADQUARTERS ARMIES OF THE UNITED STATES,
Washington, D.C., April 4, 1864.

Maj. Gen. W. T. SHERMAN,
Commanding Military Division of the Mississippi:

GENERAL: It is my design, if the enemy keep quiet and allow me to take the initiative in the spring campaign, to work all parts of the army together and somewhat toward a common center. For your information I now write you my programme as at present determined upon. . . . You I propose to move against Johnston's army, to break it up and to get into the interior of the enemy's country as far as you can, inflicting all the damage you can against their war resources.

I do not propose to lay down for you a plan of campaign, but simply to lay down the work it is desirable to have done, and leave you free to execute in your own way. Submit to me, however, as early as you can, your plan of operations. . . . I want to be ready to move by the 25th instant if possible; but all I can now direct is that you get ready as soon as possible. I know you will have difficulties to encounter getting through the mountains to where supplies are abundant, but I believe you will accomplish it. . . .

I am, general, very respectfully, your obedient servant,

U. S. GRANT,
Lieutenant-General[5]

HEADQUARTERS ARMIES OF THE UNITED STATES,
Culpepper Court-House, Va., April 19, 1864.

Maj. Gen. W. T. SHERMAN,
Commanding Military Division of the Mississippi:

GENERAL: Since my letter of April 4th I have seen no reason to change any portion of the general plan of campaign. . . . I think Saturday, the 30th, will probably be the day for our general move.
. . . [I]f the two main attacks, yours and the one from here, should promise great success, the enemy may, in a fit of desperation, abandon one part of their line of defense, and throw their whole strength upon a single army. . . .
. . . My directions, then, would be, if the enemy in your front show signs of joining Lee, follow him up to the full extent of your ability. . .

U. S. GRANT,
Lieutenant-General[6]

CULPEPPER, VA., April 28, 1864-11 PM
(Received 1.40 AM, 29th.)

Major-General SHERMAN:

Get your forces up so as to move by the 5th of May.

U. S. GRANT,
Lieutenant-General[7]

---

* The term "line of operations" is from Jomini, who defined strategic lines as "those lines which the army would follow to reach one of these decisive points or to accomplish an important maneuver." See, for instance, J. D. Hittle (ed.), *Jomini and His Summary of the Art of War* (Harrisburg, Penn.: Stackpole Books, 1952). Civil War generals were familiar with Jomini, and the contemporary literature is replete with Jominian terms.

The blank table following this is for those who would like to try their hand at determining Sherman's mission before looking at the author's solution. A glance at figure 4.1 and map 5.2 may help.

TABLE 5.2 *Worksheet for Sherman's Tasks*

Task Description	Task Purpose/Source	Priority	Type*

* Specified task (S) or implied task (I).

Sherman's restated mission is:

_____

_____

_____

_____

_____

_____

_____

_____

_____

_____

_____

_____

Desired end state:

_____

_____

_____

_____

_____

_____

_____

_____

_____

_____

_____

MAP 5.1 *Lines of Operation*

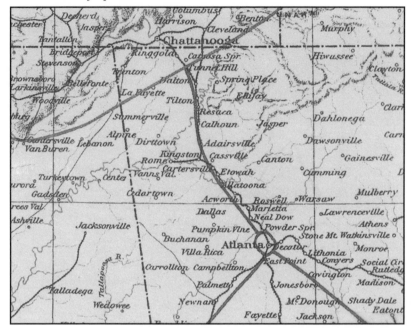

The author's solution is shown in Table 5.3.

Sherman's restated mission is:

Attack not later than 5 May 1864 to break up Johnston's army. Advance towards Atlanta in order to deny the enemy the resources of the country. Pursue Johnston's army if it attempts to join Lee. As necessary, cross major rivers, preserve and extend lines of communications, and take Atlanta.

Desired end state: Johnston's army rendered militarily ineffective and the war resources of Georgia destroyed or denied to the Confederacy.

More tasks—in particular, intermediate tasks—could be found. The preservation of rail lines of communication (supply lines) is implied, because they were essential in the absence of waterborne lines of communication; the Union Army in Chattanooga had almost starved the previous fall when both river and rail resupply lines broke down.

TABLE 5.3 *Sherman's Tasks*

Task Description	Task Purpose/Source	Priority	Type
1. Break up Johnston's army.	Destroy the military capability of the opposing army (4 April letter)	1	S
2. Get into the interior of the country and damage war resources.	Deny the country's war resources to the enemy (4 April letter)	2	S
3. Protect, extend, and maintain rail lines of communication.	Keep army in a supply condition to maneuver, attack, and pursue	3	I
4. Prepare to pursue Johnston if he attempts to join Lee.	Prevent or penalize any attempt by the Confederate government to reinforce Lee in Virginia to defeat Grant (19 April letter)	4	S
5. Start movement on or by 5 May 1864.	Synchronize operations with those in Virginia (28 April letter)	5	S
6. Conduct river-crossing operations.	Cross Oostanaula, Etowah, and Chattahoochee Rivers; support task 2 (map 2)	6	I
7. Take Atlanta.	Support task 2 (map 1)	7	I

In Archer Jones's terms (see chapter 3), Sherman is being directed to adopt an offensive (attack) combat ("break up" Johnston's army) persisting (get into the interior of the country) operational mode. He is then to adopt an offensive logistic operational mode ("inflicting all the damage you can against their war resources"). General Grant has also defined for General Sherman those elements of the Confederacy he considers to be "centers of gravity"* in Sherman's theater: Johnston's army and the war resources in the interior of Georgia. Although not following a modern format, Grant provided the essential instructions Sherman needed.

---

* Centers of gravity are those characteristics, capabilities, or localities from which a military force derives its freedom of action, physical strength, or will to fight. From Joint Publication 1-02, *The DOD Dictionary of Military and Associated Terms* (Washington, D.C.: Department of Defense, 1994).

Map 5.2 *The Campaign Area*

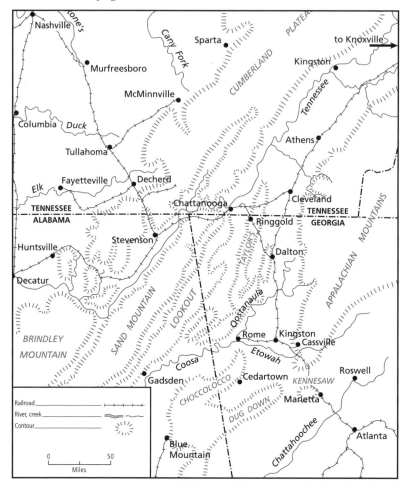

END-OF-CHAPTER NOTES

1. Joint Publication 1-02, *The DOD Dictionary of Military and Associated Terms* (Washington, D.C.: Department of Defense, 1994), 271.
2. FM 101-5, *Staff Organization and Operations* (Washington, D.C.: Department of the Army, 1984), G-86-87.
3. William T. Sherman, *Memoirs of General William T. Sherman* (New York: Da Capo Press, Inc., 1984), Volume II, 5–6.
4. Albert Casteel, *Decision in the West: The Atlanta Campaign of 1864* (Lawrence, Kansas: University of Kansas Press, 1992), 67–68.
5. 32 *OR* 3:245.
6. 32 *OR* 3:409.
7. 32 *OR* 3:521.
8. 32 *OR* 3:261.

CHAPTER 6

Sherman's Considerations

ESTIMATE OF THE SITUATION

I. MISSION

II. THE SITUATION AND COURSES OF ACTION

A. *Situation Analysis*

(1) Geostrategic Context

    (a) Domestic and International Context

    (b) Characteristics of the Operational Area

(2) Analysis of the Enemy

    (a) Broad Courses of Action

    (b) Political and Military Intentions and Objectives

    (c) Military Strategic and Operational Advantages and Limitations

    (d) Possible External Military Support

    (e) Centers of Gravity

    (f) Specific Operational Characteristics (strength, composition, location and disposition, reinforcements, logistics, time and space factors, and combat efficiency)

(3) Friendly Situation—Same Factors as Used for Enemy

(4) Assumptions

(5) Deductions—Relative Combat Power

B. *Course of Action Development*

III. ANALYSIS OF OPPOSING COURSES OF ACTION

IV. COMPARISON OF OWN COURSES OF ACTION

V. DECISION

T his chapter addresses facts about the geographical area of operations, the Confederate Army, and the Union Army from
Sherman's viewpoint. Section 2(A)(1)(a) of the situation estimate
outline, the domestic and international context, is covered by chapter 4.
The following data is all taken from the messages and other information
known to be available to Sherman. It is *not necessarily correct* in all respects,
but expresses Sherman's beliefs, as reflected in his correspondence prior
to the campaign.

CHARACTERISTICS OF THE OPERATIONAL AREA
Military Geography

Map 5.2 clearly illustrates the topographic characteristics of the area. In
the western two-thirds of the area, there are the long ridges of the
Cumberland Plateau in the west and the Ridge and Valley region in the
center of the map, all trending northeast to southwest. These ridges all
have steep sides, and the Cumberland Plateau has relatively flat tops. To
the east, the Appalachian Mountains and their extension south of the
Coosa are as steep and higher in elevation, but they lack the characteristic flat tops of the Cumberland Plateau. The valleys and some of the
plateau areas contain rich soil, under cultivation primarily for foodstuffs
during the Civil War. Corn and wheat were common crops. The movement of large bodies of troops was restricted to the valleys, plateau areas,
and to specific passes over the mountains.

Numerous streams and rivers run throughout the area, providing adequate water in all seasons. Only two rivers were navigable, but the rivers
shown on map 5.2 were not fordable except at very limited points.
Bridges served the railroads and most wagon roads led either to ferries
or fords. Pontoon trains—up to 150 wagons carrying boats and bridging
equipment—were required to cross major rivers at other than bridges or
fords, particularly in the spring or early summer. A typical pontoon
bridge is shown by photo 1.4. The Chattahoochee at Roswell was 650
feet wide.[1] The two rivers that meet south of Dalton to form the
Oostanaula River, the Conasauga and the Coosawattee, were fordable at
several places.[2]

During late spring and early summer, the weather is warm and humid.
Highs can reach the 90° Fahrenheit mark and the usual lows are in the
60s. Showers and rain are common, although after June they become
rare and intermittent streams start drying up. Daylight lasts for more

than 14 hours each day. Weather forecasting was a black art in 1864; the principal source for forecasts was the *Farmer's Almanack*. Table 6.1, which is taken from the *Almanack*, applies to Boston but a similar version may have been used by soldiers on the battlefield.

TABLE 6.1 *Extract from the* Farmer's Almanack

Month	Date	Day	Length of Day h m	Moonrise or Moonset h m	Weather Forecast
May	1	Sunday	14 8	rise 2:10	Good weather
	2	Monday	14 10	2:42	
	3	Tuesday	14 12	3:15	
	4	Wednesday	14 15	3:49	Rain
	5	Thursday	14 17	new moon	
	6	Friday	14 19	sets 8:03	
	7	Saturday	14 21	9:02	
	8	Sunday	14 23	9:54	
	9	Monday	14 26	10:40	Dull with some rain
	10	Tuesday	14 28	11:20	
	11	Wednesday	14 31	11:55	
	12	Thursday	14 33	1st quarter	
	13	Friday	14 35	12:25	
	14	Saturday	14 37	12:52	Cool
	15	Sunday	14 39	1:18	
	16	Monday	14 41	1:44	
	17	Tuesday	14 43	2:12	
	18	Wednesday	14 45	2:42	Good weather
	19	Thursday	14 47	3:15	
	20	Friday	14 49	3:52	
	21	Saturday	14 50	full moon	
	22	Sunday	14 52	rises 8:38	
	23	Monday	14 54	9:32	
	24	Tuesday	14 55	10:20	High winds
	25	Wednesday	14 57	11:02	Good weather
	26	Thursday	14 58	11:39	
	27	Friday	14 59	last quarter	
	28	Saturday	15 1	12:13	
	29	Sunday	15 3	12:45	
	30	Monday	15 3	1:17	
	31	Tuesday	15 5	1:50	

continued

TABLE 6.1 *Extract from the* Farmer's Almanack, *continued*

Month	Date	Day	Length of Day h m	Moonrise or Moonset h m	Weather Forecast
June	1	Wednesday	15 6	2:25	
	2	Thursday	15 7	3:03	Showers
	3	Friday	15 8	3:47	
	4	Saturday	15 9	new moon	
	5	Sunday	15 11	sets 8:34	
	6	Monday	15 11	9:17	
	7	Tuesday	15 12	9:58	Good weather
	8	Wednesday	15 12	10:25	
	9	Thursday	15 14	10:54	
	10	Friday	15 14	11:21	
	11	Saturday	15 15	11:47	
	12	Sunday	15 15	1st quarter	Variable
	13	Monday	15 16	12:14	
	14	Tuesday	15 16	12:42	
	15	Wednesday	15 16	1:12	
	16	Thursday	15 17	1:45	
	17	Friday	15 17	2:25	Good weather
	18	Saturday	15 17	3:14	
	19	Sunday	15 17	full moon	
	20	Monday	15 17	rises 8:14	
	21	Tuesday	15 17	8:59	
	22	Wednesday	15 16	9:39	
	23	Thursday	15 16	10:15	
	24	Friday	15 16	10:48	
	25	Saturday	15 15	11:20	
	26	Sunday	15 15	11:53	
	27	Monday	15 15	last quarter	
	28	Tuesday	15 14	12:27	
	29	Wednesday	15 14	1:04	
	30	Thursday	15 13	1:45	

The ground was (in general) favorable to the defense. The Union bases were at Nashville and Chattanooga, and the Confederate base was more than 100 miles southeast of Chattanooga. The long mountain ridges interspersed with rivers provided successive barriers to the movement of troops northwest to southeast (Chattanooga to Atlanta). The

PHOTO 6.1 *View of Ringgold, Georgia, in 1864, taken from the west and showing Ringgold Gap in the distance.* PHOTO ARC 524949, NATIONAL ARCHIVES

ridges also protected and concealed lateral (northeast to southwest or vice versa) movement. Photo 6.1 shows the town of Ringgold, with White Oak Mountain and Taylor's Ridge beyond, illustrating the nature of the mountainous terrain. Weather conditions were to be good for campaigning, although frequent rains would bog the roads down, slowing movement.

Transportation

RAILWAYS

Five railroads were key to the campaign, supplying the essentials to both armies. The roads, cars, and locomotives were in varying states of repair; those maintained by the South were in relatively poor condition.

The railroad leading from Atlanta to Chattanooga—the Western and Atlantic Railroad, 138 miles between the two cities—provided most of Johnston's supplies. Some supplies came by way of the Selma and Rome Railroad, which was completed only from Selma in western Alabama to Blue Mountain, 25 miles south of Gadsden and just north of present-day

Anniston. The distance from Blue Mountain to Rome was 60 miles, which took the stagecoach 12 hours to cover. The Rome Railroad connected Rome to the Western and Atlantic at Kingston, Georgia, with two trains daily.[3] Based on a resupply requirement of 13 pounds per day per man and an estimate of 60,000 men under arms, Johnston needed about four 10-car trains each day from the Western and Atlantic. A key point on this railway, the tunnel at Tunnel Hill, is shown in photo 6.2. The tunnel was actually just behind the screening position of General Wheeler's Confederate cavalry at the start of the campaign, and therefore was not important to the Confederates unless they were successful in defeating Sherman and then attacking north. It was vital for Sherman to capture it intact if he planned to use the railroad for supplies as he moved toward Atlanta.

Sherman depended on three rail lines. The Nashville and Chattanooga connected those two cities and was the most direct route between his major supply base at Nashville and the army. It was inadequate to the task, however, and the Central Alabama Railroad (Nashville to Decatur) and the Memphis and Charleston Railroad (Decatur to Stevenson, where it joined

PHOTO 6.2 *The Western & Atlantic railroad tunnel at Tunnel Hill, Georgia, in 1864. The tunnel is still there, paralleled by a more modern one.* PHOTO ARC 530351, NATIONAL ARCHIVES

the Nashville and Chattanooga) were used by Sherman to take up the slack. Even then, he estimated that the supplies would be barely adequate for his force.[4] With maximum effort, the railroad was able to supply the army and accumulate an additional day's supplies at Chattanooga on each day.[5]

The other railroad on the map, the Eastern Tennessee and Georgia Railroad leading north from Dalton, passed through Union territory before leading back into Confederate territory in Virginia. It was not important to the campaign, except initially in moving some Union troops from Knoxville south towards Dalton.

ROAD WAGONS

Most roads indicated in map 6.1 were narrow dirt tracks, suitable for the movement of troops and cavalry but liable to break down under heavy use and during wet weather. Wagon loads of less than 3,000 pounds were recommended, except on the main road paralleling the railroad between Chattanooga and Atlanta and on the road to Rome. These two roads were in better condition than average and could sustain heavier loads. Most roads would sustain the march of only one army corps per day—more than that could not fit on the road unless the supply trains were left behind.[6]

RIVERS

There are two navigable rivers in the area: the Tennessee and the Coosa (see map 5.2). In 1864, the Tennessee was navigable in most seasons from the Ohio River to the western edge of Alabama. There, Mussel Shoals rendered the river impassable except during very high water. Above the shoals, the river was again navigable all the way to Knoxville, Tennessee, although between Stevenson and Chattanooga—where the river passes through the Cumberland Plateau—the current was swift and treacherous. The Union maintained riverboat fleets, including gunboats, on both sides of Mussel (now Muscle) Shoals. An additional route of supply for Sherman was the use of the Tennessee River to Johnsonville, Tennessee, where stores were transshipped to the railroad leading east to Nashville. After the end of the campaign (2 November 1864), Major General Nathan Bedford Forrest managed to cause significant damage to the supplies there.

The Coosa, a smaller stream, was navigable from below Gadsden to Rome. Several small riverboats such as the steamers *Alfaretta* and *Laura Moore* served the Confederacy on this stretch.[7] The river below

MAP 6.1 *Wagon Road Network*

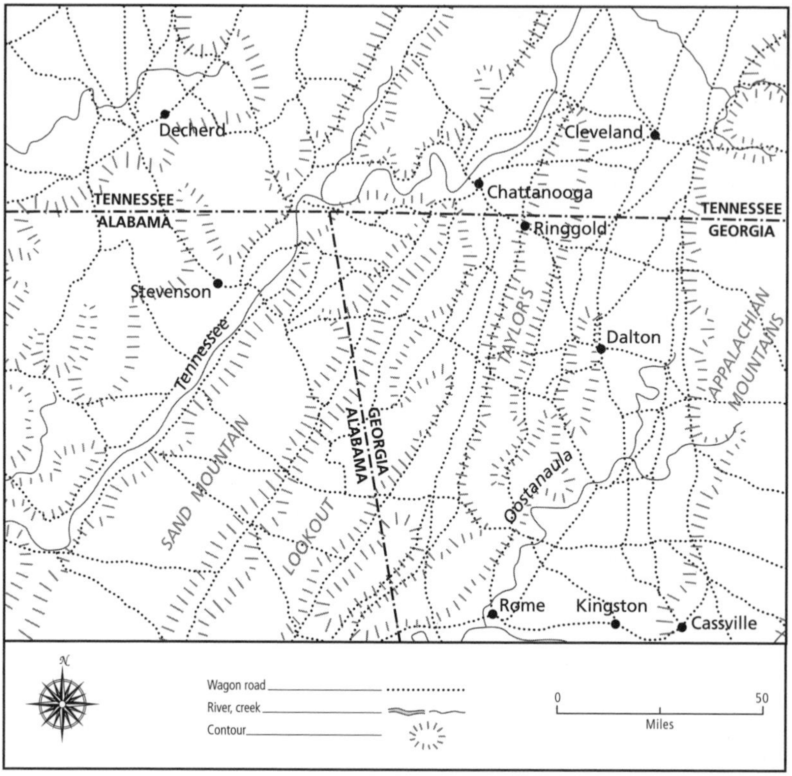

Gadsden was not navigable due to a series of shoals. River width was 300 to 400 feet (about 100 meters).[8]

Economics

In 1864 there were two significant spheres of economic activity in northwest Georgia: agriculture and heavy industry. Predominantly, the area was (and is) agricultural. Depending on the exact land and soil type involved, corn yields were 5 to 12 barrels per acre or 6 to 50 bushels of wheat or oats per acre.[9]

During the Civil War, the primary crops were food staples—especially corn and wheat—not the cotton that had previously been a major crop. Since the beginning of the war, local farmers raised much more food—double the previous amount of corn—and less cotton. Rye, barley, apples, onions, sweet potatoes, Irish potatoes, tomatoes, okra, peppers, beets, pumpkins, and peaches were all being grown. Horses, beef cattle, and sheep were raised on the plentiful grazing lands. There was an acute shortage of salt and, with the nearness of the armies and their foraging parties, the country was being stripped of its seed stores and breeding stock.[10] According to one of Sherman's agents, "everything north of Atlanta is virtually skinned."[11]

In northern Georgia, corn was planted in March and could be harvested for "roasting ears" as early as June, although generally the crop was not ready until July. Winter wheat was planted in the fall, the fields grazed until late winter, then allowed to grow out for harvest in the late spring and early summer.[12]

The spring of 1864 was cold and wet. Late freezes killed many garden vegetables, nearly all plums and peaches, and some apples. There was a good stand of wheat in early April, not yet mature.[13] Several late frosts and wet weather had caused the March corn planting to rot in the ground; it had to be replanted in April, meaning late, reduced yields. Wheat and oats were safe in late April but not yet ready to be harvested—there was some concern about wheat rust damaging the crop.[14] As the armies began their campaign there was the prospect of an adequate cereal and fruit crop, and the grass was growing long for foraging animals.[15]

There were industrial plants producing war goods for the Confederacy in Rome, along the Etowah River, and in Atlanta itself. In Rome there was the Noble & Co. Ironworks and Machine Shop, an important armaments factory. Along the north bank of the Etowah River east of Cassville was the Etowah Iron Works. Near Roswell on the Chattahoochee were cotton, wool, and paper mills.[16] Most important, Atlanta was not only a transportation hub but also a major industrial and supply center. There were an arsenal manufacturing military goods; several rifle, pistol, and cannon foundries; gristmills; flour mills; meat-packing plants; and hospitals. Atlanta was the logistics center of the Deep South.[17]

Sociology

According to the 1860 census,[18] the northern Georgia population consisted primarily of small farmers scattered throughout the region, with a significant number of prosperous farmers and some plantations, many located in the Etowah Valley. Short of Atlanta itself, a large and wealthy rail junction town of 9,551 (an 1860 figure, probably much larger in 1864, considering the war buildup), the most important center in the region was Rome, a town of 4,000 with extensive shops and industries.

Other significant towns, primarily acting as agricultural markets, included Dalton, Kingston, Cassville, Marietta, and Cedartown. The county populations ranged from 15,724 in Cass County (Cassville), 15,195 in Floyd County (Rome), and 14,242 in Cobb County (Marietta) to 5,082 in Catoosa County (Ringgold). Population densities ranged from 20 per-square mile in Polk County (Cedartown) to 42 per square mile in Cobb County.

Of the total 1860 population in the nine-county area of northwest Georgia (85,292), about 75 percent was white. The majority of the population—except slaves—could be expected to be in sympathy to the South, even to the extent of mounting small guerrilla attacks against Union supply lines. Most would provide information to the Confederacy, but a small percentage would support and provide information to Union soldiers.

ANALYSIS OF THE ENEMY

Broad Courses of Action

The Confederate army under General Joseph Eggleston Johnston (photo 6.3), in spite of being outnumbered, had some freedom of action and could attack, defend, or perform a retrograde operation. Attacks were primarily possible against forward elements of the Union Army, particularly if some of these elements moved out of supporting distance from the rest, allowing the Confederate Army to attain a local superiority. Attacks against Union supply lines could also be expected. The Confederates had constructed some fortifications around the Dalton area, indicating a capability and possibly an intention to defend there. The terrain, mountainous with numerous rivers, was also advantageous for a delay. Equally easily, Johnston's army could withdraw to other favorable positions or to reinforce other Confederate armies elsewhere. Conversely, Johnston could be reinforced from other Confederate armies and therefore potentially could field manpower close to that of the Union Army. A detailed analysis of Johnston's capabilities is deferred until the next chapter.

Political and Military Intentions and Objectives

The principal political objectives of the Confederacy were independence and the removal of Union forces from the territory of the Confederate

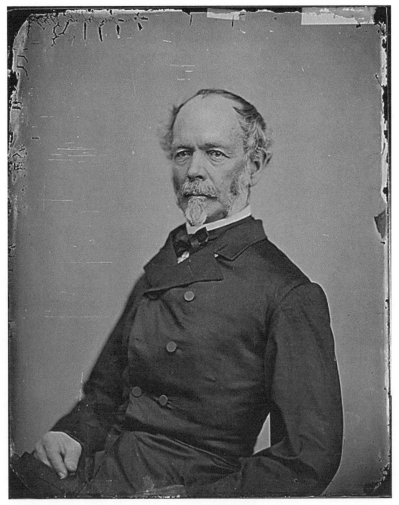

PHOTO 6.3 *General Joseph E. Johnston, Commanding General of the Confederate Army of Tennessee.* PHOTO ARC 525983, NATIONAL ARCHIVES

states. The primary military objective of Confederate armies was to decisively defeat Union forces in the field, causing their retreat and eventual removal from Confederate territory. Given the disparity of forces involved, a more realistic objective was to not lose a major battle or a vital area, hoping to exhaust the Union will. It was believed that a significant Confederate military success, or at least no major failure, would so affect the morale of the North's voters that the elections in the fall of 1864 would bring peace candidates to power.

Military Strategic and Operational Advantages and Limitations

The Confederacy had both advantages and disadvantages at this stage of the war. Its principal advantage was its war objective—the Confederacy could win just by not losing. Operationally, it had the support of the populace in the area being fought over, its supply lines were relatively short, and the terrain was favorable for defense. Its important limitations were the enormous disparity in manpower and resources (its soldiers being outnumbered better than two to one in the theater of operations alone) and the proximity of the Union Army to vital war resources in Georgia that the Confederate Army had to protect. The vulnerability of these resources made it difficult for Johnston to overcome the manpower and materiel disparity through innovative maneuver.

Possible External Military Support

By this stage of the war, the Confederacy's earlier hopes of British and French intervention had almost disappeared. In any case, their intervention probably would have been limited to naval actions lifting the blockade and—even if it had occurred in the spring of 1864—such an intervention would have had little measurable effect in north Georgia.

Centers of Gravity

As explained in the previous chapter, centers of gravity are those characteristics, capabilities, or localities from which a military force derives its freedom of action, physical strength, or will to fight. General Grant specified for General Sherman the elements of the Confederacy that he considered to be "centers of gravity" in Sherman's theater: Johnston's army and the war resources in the interior of Georgia. As long as the Confederacy had creditable armies and the ability to support them, there would be no victory for the Union army.

Specific Operational Characteristics

STRENGTH AND COMPOSITION

According to reports, the strength of the Confederate army in and around Dalton was between 40,000 and 60,000 soldiers; probably approximately 40,000 infantry, 10,000 cavalry, and 160 cannon. It was organized into two infantry corps under Lieutenant General John Bell Hood (photo 6.4), with three or four divisions, and Lieutenant General

William J. Hardee (photo 6.5), with four or five divisions. Part of Lieutenant General Leonidas Polk's (photo 6.6) army from Mississippi was reported to be present. Hood's division commanders (all major generals except Johnson, a brigadier general) were Carter L. Stevenson, Alexander P. Stewart, Thomas C. Hindman, and possibly Bushrod Johnson. Hardee's division commanders (major generals) were Benjamin F. Cheatham, Patrick R. Cleburne, William H. T. Walker, and William B. Bate. Each division had three four-gun batteries of artillery attached. A small brigade under Brigadier General John C. Brown with 1,200 men was at Rome. State troops, up to 10,000 in number, guarded the railroad and bridges around Kingston and Cartersville (just south of Cassville). A cavalry division under Major General Joseph Wheeler (photo 6.7) was screening the front of the army, another under Brigadier General William T. Martin was at Blue Mountain, Alabama, and a third was resting in the right rear of the army. A separate division of 5,000 to 7,000 men—not included in the Dalton strength—was in northern Alabama under General Philip D. Roddey, screening the Tennessee River from positions along its south bank.[19]

LOCATION AND DISPOSITION

Map 6.2 shows the dispositions that Sherman believed Confederate units occupied. Additionally, extensive fortifications, including a dam capable of flooding the pass, were reported at Buzzard's Roost (the gap in Rocky Face Ridge just west of Dalton). More fortifications were at Rome (two on the north bank, one on the south), on the north bank of the river at Resaca, and at the railroad bridges across the Etowah and the Chattahoochee.[20]

REINFORCEMENT

Reinforcements available to Johnston and their locations were:
- Polk's Corps (10,000 effectives)
  - Major General William W. Loring's Division at Centerville (central Alabama) or Blue Mountain, Alabama
  - Major General Samuel G. French's Division at Demopolis, Alabama (far west portion of Alabama)
- Major General Stephen D. Lee's Cavalry (10,000 effectives) in two commands
  - Lee's Command in north Mississippi
  - Forrest's Command raiding in west Tennessee

MAP 6.2 *Confederate Dispositions*

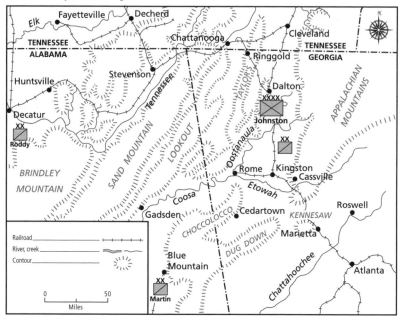

LOGISTICS

As of 7 March, the Confederate army was on short rations, with only two week's supplies on hand. Artillery horses were in bad condition.[21] By early April, matters were a little better. Quartermaster officers had supplied 1,000 loaded wagons and 1,000 good artillery horses to the army. The countryside north of Atlanta had little surplus food or forage, but the army was being supplied from southern and central Alabama and Mississippi. Depots were established at Atlanta and at Blue Mountain—the 1864 terminus of the Selma to Rome railroad, 25 miles south of Gadsden.[22]

TIME AND SPACE FACTORS

The main Confederate Army could attack in full strength against Union forward positions facing Dalton with little warning, measured in hours. It could redeploy against Union positions in north Alabama by train— via Mobile, Alabama, and Tupelo, Mississippi—or by road, but such a movement would take at least two weeks and would leave Atlanta uncovered. It could move by train to Virginia to reinforce General Robert E. Lee, but the move would take several weeks and would leave the entire center of the Confederacy uncovered.

PHOTO 6.4 *Lieutenant General John Bell Hood, one of General Johnston's corps commanders, shown in a postwar photograph.* PHOTO ARC 529378, NATIONAL ARCHIVES

PHOTO 6.5 *Lieutenant General William J. Hardee, senior corps commander in the Army of Tennessee.* PHOTO LC-USZ62-14973, LIBRARY OF CONGRESS

PHOTO 6.6 *Lieutenant General Leonidas Polk, Commanding General of the Army of Mississippi, which joined Johnston and became Polk's Corps, Army of Tennessee.* PHOTO LC-DIG-CWPB-06714 DLC, LIBRARY OF CONGRESS

Polk's Corps, using a combination of marching and railroads, could reinforce Johnston in one to two weeks. Major General S. D. Lee's cavalry, on the other hand, would probably raid Union supply lines rather than join Johnston. Within one week they could be astride either the Central Alabama or the Nashville and Chattanooga Railroads in Tennessee.

Combat Efficiency

Some reports doubted the Confederate Army's morale, a civilian line-crosser stating "force . . . constantly diminishing by sickness, desertion, &c."[23] and an agent reporting that "[e]very point he was at he saw gangs of deserters at work in chains, and met them on all trains; the slave exemptions creating a good deal of bitter feeling."[24] Other agents believed the army to have relatively high efficiency: "I consider General Johnston's army in as good condition to-day as Bragg's army ever was."[25]

ANALYSIS OF THE UNION POSITION

Broad Courses of Action

General Sherman had significant freedom of action in the way he might choose to attack, but attack he must. Because General Grant desired the destruction of both Johnston's army and the war resources of Georgia, the attack must engage that army and lead towards Atlanta. Any maneuver towards these ends was possible. Detailed course of action development for the Union Army will take place in chapter 8.

Political and Military Intentions and Objectives

The principal political objective of the Union was to force the Confederate states to rejoin the Union on terms guaranteeing the primacy of the federal government over that of the states. The abolition of slavery was desired but was not an absolute objective, even this late in the war and in spite of the Emancipation Proclamation. To this political end, the Union military was to destroy the entities opposing the federal government: Confederate armies and their supporting infrastructure, including government. In this theater, that objective meant destroying Johnston's army and war resources in Georgia, much of the latter being in the Atlanta area.

Military Strategic and Operational Advantages and Limitations

The Union also had significant advantages and disadvantages at this stage of the war. Its principal advantage was its overwhelming superiority in manpower and in the industrial infrastructure essential to modern war. Additionally, it had split the Confederacy along the Mississippi and had effective control of large areas nominally Confederate, including the important cities of New Orleans and Nashville. Operationally, it had the initiative and superiority of numbers and materiel at the point of attack. It was close to vital areas Johnston must defend.

The Union Army's important limitations were the necessity to win convincingly prior to the fall elections and its long and vulnerable supply line. Although the terrain was favorable to defense, its complexity made numerous opportunities for operational maneuver available.

Possible External Military Support

No external support was probable.

Centers of Gravity

The Union strategic center of gravity was the morale of the populace. After three years of war and appalling casualty lists, widespread perception was that the war was a stalemate. Unless progress was made and morale rejuvenated, presidential elections in the autumn could result in a peace candidate being elected.

The operational center of gravity of Sherman's army was its supply line. Although there were ample stores in Chattanooga and Nashville, the army had no hope of living off the land. A three-day cessation in supplies delivered after a battle or 20 days without resupply—even with no battle being fought—would result in retreat or even a major defeat.

Specific Operational Characteristics

STRENGTH AND COMPOSITION

According to official returns dated 30 April 1864 and supporting messages, the strength of the Union Army that Sherman could commit to the campaign was about 120,000 men. Sherman, in a letter written on 4 May, apparently counted only infantry and grossly undercounted the Army of the Cumberland, for unknown reasons. He listed Thomas as having 45,000; McPherson, 20,000; and Schofield, 13,000; for a total of 78,000.[26] In his memoirs, Sherman cited a figure as of 1 May of 98,797 men and 254 guns—Thomas, 60,773 and 130 guns; McPherson, 24,465 and 96 guns; and Schofield, 13,559 and 28 guns—but gave no source.[27] Table 6.2 is a list of the units and their approximate strengths drawn from the *Official Records* (source pages shown in table). Strengths include all those present; some were undoubtedly sick or ineffective for other reasons.

LOCATION AND DISPOSITION

Map 6.3 illustrates Union troop locations as of 30 April 1864.

REINFORCEMENT

Potential reinforcements for Sherman as of 30 April included:

PHOTO 6.7 *Major General Joseph Wheeler, commanding the Cavalry Corps of the Army of Tennessee. The picture was taken after his promotion to lieutenant general.* PHOTO ARC 529234, NATIONAL ARCHIVES

- Brigadier General Kenner Garrard's cavalry division at Columbia, Tennessee (6,678 present, 3,500 effective, 6 cannon) [28]
- Brigadier General J. E. Smith's 3rd division, XVth Corps, and attached cavalry regiment protecting the rail lines at Huntsville, Alabama (3,678 present, 8 cannon)[29]
- Major General Frank Blair's XVIIth Corps, returning from leave at Cairo, Illinois (10,000 effective, 42 cannon)[30]
- Major General George Stoneman's cavalry division at Nicholasville, Kentucky (3,688 present, 3,810 effectives)[31]

Garrard's and Stoneman's cavalry divisions were under orders to join the campaign as soon as possible, and the infantry divisions were expected to join at a later date.

LOGISTICS

The armies were well supplied in all respects except in terms of cavalry horses. Seventy days' supplies for 100,000 men were at the forward depots around Chattanooga and Decatur, the armies had between 10 and

TABLE 6.2 *Composition and Strength of the Union Army*

Unit	Commander	Present for Duty	Cannon	Source
Army of the Cumberland	Thomas		32	OR 3:550
Headquarters		848		
IV Corps (3 div)	Howard	21,138	30	
XIV Corps (3 div)	Palmer	23,804	36	
XX Corps (3 div)	Hooker	22,019	36	
Army of the Tennessee	McPherson			32 OR 3:534
Headquarters		34		32 OR 3:561
XV Corps (3 div)	Logan	13,235	30	
XVI Corps (2 div)	Dodge	12,886	30	
Army of the Ohio	Schofield			
Headquarters		47		32 OR 3:533
XXIII Corps (3 div)	Schofield	12,040	24	32 OR 3:569
Cavalry Corps (2 div)	Elliot	7,988	6	32 v 3:550
Engineer troops (3 bde)		3,377		32 OR 3:550
Unassigned		2,942		
TOTAL	Sherman	120,358	192	

20 days' supplies in their possession, and the depot at Nashville contained supplies for six months. The rail lines supported more than 100,000 men and allowed one day's accumulation each day at Chattanooga as well as the day's current consumption. Cavalry horses were being supplied at only half the required rate to the two reinforcing cavalry divisions of Garrard and Stoneman.[32]

TIME AND SPACE FACTORS

Each of the three armies was disposed differently and required different assembly and movement times. The Army of the Cumberland was immediately ready to conduct operations in the Dalton area. Each corps could move on roads in the area at a pace of about 15 miles per day, and most corps were not much farther than that from the Confederate army.

Prior to 29 April, when Sherman gave the order to move, the Army of the Tennessee was located in northern Alabama. It could move against the Confederate army in two ways: either up the railroad to the Chattanooga area and then against Dalton, taking about one week,[33] or cross-country from Huntsville to Rome. The route across the mountains could take up to two weeks, with the army needing food and forage at the end of the march. Additionally, this army could raid south into central Alabama, but supplies would be a great difficulty, due to the lack of a supporting railroad south of the Tennessee River and the low population density of the area, limiting foraging.

MAP 6.3 *Union Dispositions*

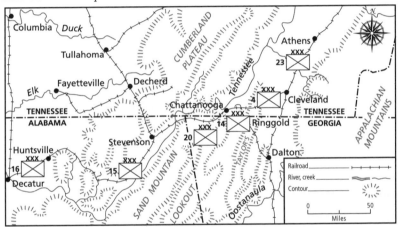

Prior to 23 April, when Sherman gave Schofield orders to move, the Army of the Ohio was dispersed around and north of Knoxville, Tennessee. To move to the Dalton area would take about one week, but Schofield would need sufficient warning—several days—to destroy the railroad into Virginia in order to prevent Confederate forces in Virginia from attacking towards Knoxville. Alternatively, Schofield could use the same railroad to attack into southwestern Virginia, but such an attack would take his army out of this campaign.

The cavalry reinforcements were expected in the Dalton area by the second week in May, but infantry reinforcements would take longer—the exact delay difficult to estimate—because those units were still receiving their men back from furlough.

TABLE 6.3 *Relative Combat Power*

Function	Advantage	Rationale
Intelligence	Significant Confederate	Superior cavalry (10,000 compared to 8,000 plus 10,000 reinforcements versus 7,500; and a qualitative advantage) and support of the majority of civilians in area.
Maneuver	Overwhelming Union	Infantry strength advantage 5 to 2.
Fire support	Significant Union	192 guns versus 160 plus Union qualitative advantage.
Mobility/ survivability	Slight Confederate	Less baggage—all forces move a little quicker. Interior lines. Some prepared fortifications.
Logistics	Slight Union	Much more and higher quality of supplies partially balanced by vulnerability of supply lines.
Battle command	Even	As far as Sherman knows, Johnston and his subordinates are all highly capable.
Aggregate	Significant Union	

Combat Efficiency

With the exception of part of the Army of Ohio, composed of relatively inexperienced soldiers, the Union armies were combat experienced and hardened. To quote one division commander from the Army of the Cumberland, Baird, "I think I can whip a large force. . . . My men are in fine spirits."[34] An exception to this generalization was in that cavalry, where Sherman thought "the enemy, being superior to us in cavalry at all points, . . . will [attack] our lines of communication."[35]

ASSUMPTIONS

Assumptions are intrinsically important factors upon which the conduct of the operation will be based. Sherman made at least two:

1. "Of course the movement in Virginia is the principal and ours is secondary and must conform."[36]

2. "Johnston will be compelled to hang on to his railroad, the only possible avenue of supply to his army."[37]

DEDUCTIONS: RELATIVE COMBAT POWER

One way to quantify combat power is through the use of what the present day U.S Army calls "combat functions" or "battlefield operating systems." These are: intelligence, maneuver, fire support, air defense, mobility and survivability, logistics, and battle command.[38] Air defense is of no interest in the present context—the Confederate Army not having balloons—but the rest of the functions can be characterized. Table 6.3 shows one analysis based on what Sherman knew or might have thought.

An aid like table 6.3 (used by the modern U.S. Army but of course not available to Sherman) hints at what might be possible or not. For instance, the Confederate superiority in intelligence and mobility would seem to rule out the possibility of surprising Johnston's army or of a successful tactical or operational maneuver that would put Johnston at a serious disadvantage. On the other hand, Union superiority was not so great as to allow frontal attacks against prepared positions. A reasonable course might be to use part of the army to fix the Confederate Army and maneuver with the rest. This approach might cause Johnston to retreat and at least could bring him out of his fortifications, where superior Union manpower and firepower can have the most effect. However, each part of the army must be strong enough to withstand an attack by the entire Confederate Army long enough to allow the rest (which cannot be too far away) to join the fight.

END-OF-CHAPTER NOTES

1. Jacob D. Cox, *Atlanta* (Dayton, Ohio: Morningside House, Inc., 1987), 142.
2. *32 OR* 3:12.
3. Advertisements in the Rome *Tri-Weekly Courier*, Vol. 4, Nos. 102 and 113, 1 Sept. 1863 and 26 Sept. 1863.
4. *32 OR* 3:311.
5. *32 OR* 3:466.
6. Griffith, *Battle in the Civil War*, 8.
7. Advertisements in the Rome *Tri-Weekly Courier*, Vol. 5, No. 31, 12 March 1864.
8. *32 OR* 3:334.
9. George White, *Statistics of the State of Georgia* (Savannah, Georgia: W. Thorne Williams, 1849, reprinted 1972), 37.
10. Willard Range, *A Century of Georgia Agriculture* (Athens, Georgia: The University of Georgia Press, 1954), 39 and following.

11. 32 *OR* 3:295.
12. David P. Price, editor, *Modern Agriculture* (University Park, New Mexico: SWI Publishing, 1989), 113–5.
13. Rome *Tri-Weekly Courier*, Vol. 5, No. 40, 2 April 1864.
14. Rome *Tri-Weekly Courier*, Vol. 5, No. 48, 23 April 1864.
15. Range, 39 and following.
16. Cox, 137.
17. Albert Casteel, *Decision in the West* (Lawrence, Kansas: University of Kansas Press, 1992), 69–73.
18. J. Disturnell, *Census of the United States and Territories* (New York: American News Company, 1867), 22–3.
19. This information is compiled from 32 *OR* 4, pp. 10, 11, 17, 22, 29, 33, 62, 72, 90, 99, 100, 264, 282, 284, 294, 295, 308, 340, 342, 350, 351, 412, 423, 444, 451, 499, and 527. Numerous intelligence reports and estimates are documented in these records.
20. 32 *OR* 3:284, 32 *OR* 3:295.
21. 32 *OR* 3:100.
22. 32 *OR* 3:295.
23. 32 *OR* 3:451.
24. 32 *OR* 3:296.
25. 32 *OR* 3:351.
26. 38 *OR* 4:25.
27. Sherman, Vol. II, 23.
28. 32 *OR* 3:550, 38 *OR* 4:53.
29. 32 *OR* 3:561.
30. 32 *OR* 3:561, 38 *OR* 4:653.
31. 32 *OR* 3:569, 38 *OR* 4:48. The discrepancy of having more effectives than personne present is not explained.
32. Logistics data from 32 *OR* 3:220, 311, 323, 385, 408, 466, 509, 513, and 521.
33. 32 *OR* 3:534.
34. 32 *OR* 3:542.
35. 32 *OR* 3:504.
36. 32 *OR* 3:479.
37. 32 *OR* 3:466.
38. FM 100-5, *Operations* (Washington, D.C.: U.S. Government Printing Office, 1993), 2–12.

CHAPTER 7

Enemy Capabilities

ESTIMATE OF THE SITUATION

I.   MISSION

II. THE SITUATION AND COURSES OF ACTION

   A. *Situation Analysis*

   (1) Geostrategic Context

   (2) Analysis of the Enemy

     (a) Broad Courses of Action

     (b) . . .

   (3) Friendly Situation—Same Factors as Used for Enemy

   (4) Assumptions

   (5) Deductions—Relative Combat Power

   B. *Course of Action Development*

III. ANALYSIS OF OPPOSING COURSES OF ACTION

IV. COMPARISON OF OWN COURSES OF ACTION

V.   DECISION

E nemy capabilities include all those actions that the enemy—
in this case, the Confederate Army—can take that could affect
the situation. Each enemy capability includes what the enemy
can do, where he can do it, when the action can start, how long it will
take, and what strength can be devoted to the task. Each capability must
be obviously different from other listed capabilities. Normally, an
enemy may *attack* in any of several ways, *defend* in place, conduct a
retrograde operation (a delay, a withdrawal, or a retreat), or *reinforce*. Of
course, the enemy may combine certain actions, such as enveloping a
flank to gain an advantageous position and then defending that position.

If possible, the intelligence officer on a modern staff gives enemy capabilities a relative probability of adoption, or at least an opinion as to the enemy's intentions.

The following sections allow the reader to list, based on information in the book so far, Confederate capabilities from Sherman's point of view. A section is devoted to each type of maneuver: attack, defense, and retrograde. Maps that can be used to draw arrows to show possible Confederate maneuvers are included. Alternatively, the reader may skip on to the author's solution. Sherman's own views are also given at the end of the chapter.

An example of an enemy capability—in modern terminology—would be "defend in place along Rocky Face Ridge and eastward from its northern end across the railroad. The defense could start immediately and last indefinitely with at least seven divisions and more than 50,000 men." In tabular form, the restatement looks like this:

What	Where	When	How Long	What Strength
defend	in place	immediately	indefinitely	7+ divisions, 50,000+ men

ATTACK

In table 7.1, you can outline your own estimate as to the Confederate commander's attack capabilities based on his situation given in the previous chapter. Map 7.1 is provided for you to sketch arrows indicating probable attack axes. Draw a bold arrow on the map, then give the arrow a label such as "A1," standing for "Attack Option 1."

The author's suggested solution is provided in table 7.2 and map 7.2. Attack options A1 through A6 could be executed with two more divisions and at least 10,000 additional men from Polk's corps if a delay of up to two weeks in start time is acceptable. Options not listed were considered logistically impractical.

DEFEND

The reader should fill in table 7.3. No map is given, as the implicit assumption is that the defense will occur in place—the only options are when, how long, and in what strength. Options to attack, then defend, or to withdraw, then defend, should be listed in the "attack" or "retrograde" sections, respectively.

TABLE 7.1 *Confederate Attack Capabilities (Union View)*

What	Where	When	How Long	What Strength

MAP 7.1 *Confederate Attack Options (Reader's View)*

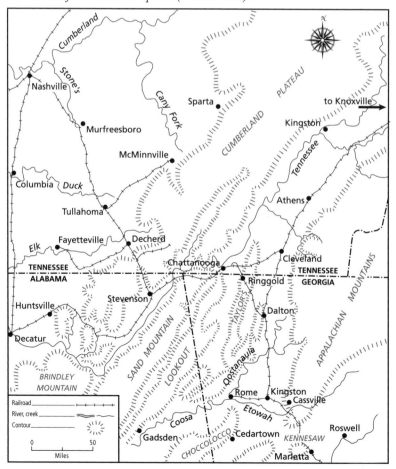

Table 7.2 *Confederate Attack Capabilities (Author's View)*

What	Where	When	How Long	What Strength
A1. Penetration	Ringgold (west towards Chattanooga)	immediately	indefinite	4+ divisions (30,000+)
A2. Penetration	north towards Cleveland	within 1 day	indefinite	4+ divisions (30,000+)
A3. Penetration	north, west of Taylor's Ridge	within 3 days	indefinite	4+ divisions (30,000+)
A4. Frontal attack (A1 + A2)	against the Army of the Cumberland	within 1 day	indefinite	7+ divisions (50,000+)
A5. Single envelopment	left flank of the center army	within 2 to 3 days	indefinite	4+ divisions (30,000+)
A6. Infiltration	between the center and left armies, on to Nashville	2 to 3 weeks	3 weeks unless capture Nashville	7+ divisions (50,000+), plus cavalry (10,000)
A7. Turning movement	by rail to Tupelo, MS, then on to Nashville	2 to 3 weeks	2 weeks after Tupelo unless seize Nashville	9 divisions (including Polk) (70,000+)
A8. Infiltration to attack supply lines	northern Mississippi into middle Tennessee	1 week	about 3 weeks	5,000+ cavalry

Table 7.3 *Confederate Defend Capabilities (Reader's View)*

What	Where	When	How Long	What Strength

MAP 7.2 *Confederate Attack Capabilities (Author's View)*

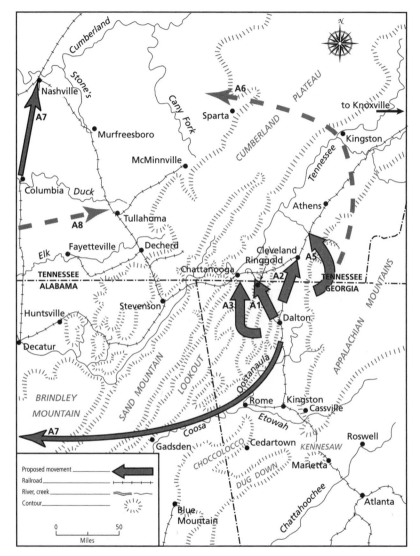

The author's solution is shown in table 7.4.

TABLE 7.4 *Confederate Defend Capabilities (Author's View)*

What	Where	When	How Long	What Strength
D1. Defend	in place	immediately	indefinitely	7+ divisions (50,000+)
D2. Defend	in place	within 2 weeks	indefinitely	9+ divisions (60,000+)

RETROGRADE

Table 7.5 and map 7.3 are for the reader's use. Remember, retrograde may include options to delay, withdraw after contact is made, or retire prior to the commencement of the campaign.

The author's solution is provided in table 7.6 and on map 7.4.

LIKELY COURSE OF ACTION

Based on what Sherman knew about Johnston's situation, the author would predict Johnston's intentions to be to defend in place, reinforced if possible (option D2), while conducting cavalry raids on lines of

MAP 7.3 *Confederate Retrograde Capabilities (Reader's View)*

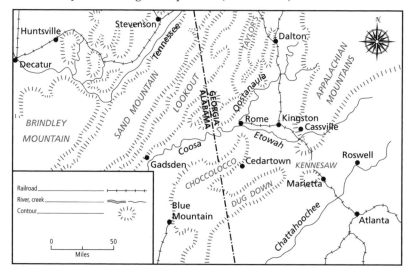

TABLE 7.5 *Confederate Retrograde Capabilities (Reader's View)*

What	Where	When	How Long	What Strength

HDQRS. MILITARY DIVISION OF THE MISSISSIPPI,
Nashville, Tenn., April 19, 1864

Major-General THOMAS,
Commanding Department of the Cumberland, Chattanooga:

GENERAL: . . .
. . . I have no apprehension of a raid on our right, for the reason
that the enemy cannot pass the Tennessee, save at isolated points,
and then only in small parties. . . .

The only real move I see for Joe Johnston is to strike your line at his
nearest point, about Cleveland or Ooltewah, but this he cannot reach
without first fighting the Ringgold force. I advise you to group your
commands so as to admit of easy and rapid concentration. . . .

W. T. SHERMAN,
Major-General, Commanding.[1]

communications (A8). Sherman himself expressed a slightly different
point of view.

SHERMAN'S OPINION

Evidence as to Sherman's estimate of Johnston's options is in Sherman's
correspondence. The quotes on pages 108-109 illustrate some of his
opinions.

Note that Sherman dismisses the author's A7 option, and states that
Johnston cannot conduct A2 without first performing A1. Ooltewah is
between Cleveland and Chattanooga, in the railroad gap through Taylor's
Ridge. He also advises Thomas as to the appropriate countermeasures.

A letter from Sherman to Grant expands on Sherman's opinion:
Sherman here mentions the author's options D1 (defense), R2 (retreat
behind the Oostanaula), and R3 (retreat behind the Etowah). The possibility of R1 (delay on successive positions) is implicit in his opinion that
Johnston will attempt to hold on to the railroad.

[CONFIDENTIAL]
HDQRS. MIL. DIV. OF THE MISSISSIPPI
Nashville, Tenn., April 24, 1864

Lieut. Gen. U. S. GRANT,
Commanding Armies of the United States, Culpeper, Va.:

GENERAL:
. . . [McPherson] will act against Johnston if he accepts battle at Dalton, or move in the direction of Rome if he gives up Dalton and falls behind the Oostenaula or Etowah. My own opinion is Johnston will be compelled to hang to his railroad, the only possible avenue of supply to his army, estimated from 45,000 to 60,000 men . . .

W. T. SHERMAN,
Major-General, Commanding.[2]

[CONFIDENTIAL]
HDQRS. MIL. DIV. OF THE MISSISSIPPI
Nashville, Tenn., April 24, 1864

Maj. Gen. J. B. MCPHERSON,
Commanding Department of the Tennessee, Huntsville:

GENERAL:
. . . The worst we have to apprehend is that Forrest may come across to act against our right flank, but this would be prevented if Washburn and Slocum threaten Grenada [Mississippi]. . . .

W. T. SHERMAN,
Major-General, Commanding.[3]

This final quote refers to attack option A8, the "worst" option as far as Sherman was concerned.

TABLE 7.6 *Confederate Retrograde Capabilities (Author's View)*

What	Where	When	How Long	What Strength
R1. **Delay on successive positions**	along the Western and Atlantic	immediately	indefinitely	7+ divisions (possible reinforcements to 9+ divisions)
R2. **Withdraw**	to the Oostanaula River	start immediately	defend in 2 days	7+ divisions (possible reinforcements to 9+ divisions)
R3. **Withdraw**	to the Etowah River— Allatoona Pass	start immediately	defend within 4 days	7+ divisions (possible reinforcements to 9+ divisions)
R4. **Withdraw**	to Kennesaw Mountain	start immediately	defend within 6 days	7+ divisions (possible reinforcements to 9+ divisions)
R5. **Withdraw**	to the Chattahoochee River	start immediately	defend within 8 days	7+ divisions (possible reinforcements to 9+ divisions)
R6. **Withdraw**	to the Atlanta defenses	start immediately	defend within 9 days	7+ divisions (possible reinforcements to 9+ divisions)
R7. **Withdraw**	to Virginia	start immediately	join Lee within 15 to 20 days	7+ divisions (possible reinforcements to 9+ divisions)

MAP 7.4 *Confederate Retrograde Capabilities (Author's View)*

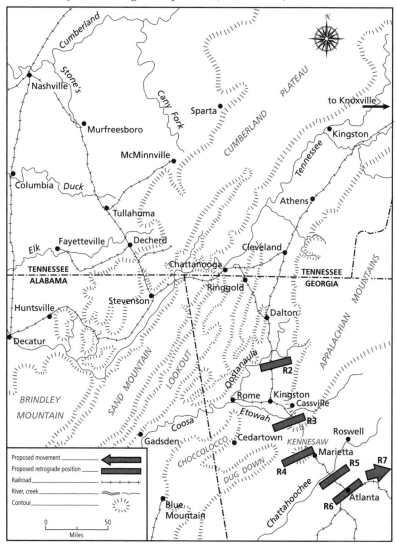

END-OF-CHAPTER NOTES

1.   32 OR 3:412.
2.   32 OR 3:466.
3.   32 OR 3:479.

CHAPTER 8

Sherman's Courses of Action

A course of action is "a possible plan open to an individual or a commander which would accomplish or is related to the accomplishment of his mission."[1] The commander normally considers several alternative courses of action before deciding upon one. The course of action must be capable of accomplishing the mission without unduly damaging the command.

MISSION

Although in theory Sherman could have attacked, defended, or performed a retrograde operation, his actions were constrained by his mission. His mission, as previously restated, was:

> **Mission:** Attack not later than 5 May 1864 to break up Johnston's army. Advance towards Atlanta in order to deny the enemy the

resources of the country. Pursue Johnston's army if it attempts to join Lee. As necessary, cross major rivers, preserve and extend lines of communications, and take Atlanta.

Desired End State: Johnston's army rendered militarily ineffective and the war resources of Georgia destroyed or denied to the Confederacy.

Accordingly, Sherman had to attack, not defend or retreat. The time to move was 5 May. Sherman made some decisions before 23 April, when he sent movement instructions to Schofield.[2] His final decision on his preferred course of action was made on 27 April and communicated to General Grant and General McPherson that day.[3] Some of the alternatives Sherman actually considered are discussed in chapter 9.

The format for outlining friendly courses of action is identical to that used for enemy capabilities in the last chapter. Courses of action must answer the questions: *what* and *how, where, when, how long,* and *what forces.* Separate courses of action must be distinguishable from each other.

READER'S COURSES OF ACTION

Below is a blank table (table 8.1) for the use of those readers who would like to list their own courses of action. A blank map (map 8.1) is also provided.

TABLE 8.1 *Attack Courses of Action (Reader's View)*

What/How	Where	When	How Long	What Forces

AUTHOR'S COURSES OF ACTION

The author's solution is provided in table 8.2 and on map 8.2. The decision as to the best course of action is discussed in chapter 11.

Map 8.1 *Sherman's Option (Reader's View)*

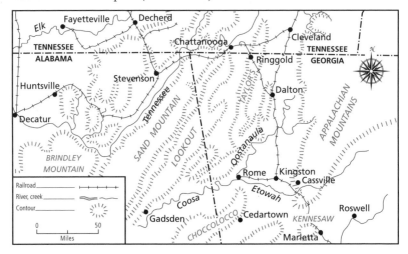

Map 8.2 *Sherman's Options (Author's View)*

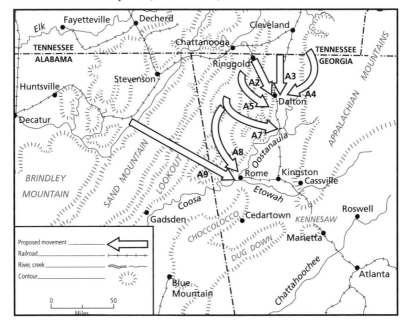

TABLE 8.2 *Attack Courses of Action (Author's View)*

What/How	Where	When	How Long	What Forces
A1. Frontal attack (map A2 + A3)	in place	a. now b. 1 to 2 weeks' prep	indefinitely	a. 3 corps (66,000) b. 6 corps (115,000)
A2. Penetration	Buzzard's Roost/ Mill Creek Gap	a. now b. 1 to 2 weeks' prep	indefinitely	a. 3 corps (66,000) b. 6 corps (115,000)
A3. Penetration	south from Red Clay (south of Cleveland)	a. now b. 1 to 2 weeks' prep	indefinitely	a. 3 corps (66,000) b. 6 corps (115,000)
A4. Single envelopment	from east of Red Clay	a. now b. 1 to 2 weeks' prep	indefinitely	a. 3 corps (66,000) b. 6 corps (115,000)
A5. Single envelopment	southern flank at Dug Gap	a. now b. 1 to 2 weeks' prep	indefinitely	a. 3 corps (66,000) b. 6 corps (115,000)
A6. Double envelopment (A4 + A5)	see above	a. now b. 1 to 2 weeks' prep	indefinitely	a. 3 corps (66,000) b. 6 corps (115,000)
A7. Shallow turning movement	through Snake Creek Gap	1 to 2 weeks' prep	20 days (until food expended)	2 to 3 corps, 3 to 4 supporting
A8. Deep turning movement	west of Taylor's Ridge to Rome	1 to 2 weeks' prep	20 days (until food expended)	2 to 3 corps, 3 to 4 supporting
A9. Very deep turning movement	cross- country to Rome	1 to 2 weeks' prep	20 days (until food expended)	2 corps (20,000) with 4 supporting

END-OF-CHAPTER NOTES

1. Field Manual 101-5, *Staff Organization and Operations* (Washington, D.C.: Department of the Army, 1984), E-4.

2. 32 *OR* 3:458.

3. 32 *OR* 3:510.

CHAPTER 9

Analysis of Courses of Action

ESTIMATE OF THE SITUATION

I.   MISSION
II. THE SITUATION AND COURSES OF ACTION
III. ANALYSIS OF OPPOSING COURSES OF ACTION
IV. COMPARISON OF OWN COURSES OF ACTION
V.   DECISION

A commander and his or her staff usually wargame* friendly courses of action against enemy capabilities. Such an analysis determines relative advantages and disadvantages among the courses of action, identifies potential improvements, and describes in more detail the measures required to put the course of action into effect. If you believe the author's choices of enemy capabilities and his choices of friendly courses of action are *all* worthy of further consideration, 153 war games are required (9 friendly courses of action times 17 enemy capabilities)! Given such a large number of analyses, it would be difficult or impossible to express each in any detail.

In most planning situations, there is very limited time available, so the commander directs that only two or three friendly courses of action—chosen by the commander—will be wargamed. He or she may even direct that only a single course of action, specified to be the commander's preferred course of action, be wargamed. Sometimes only a single enemy capability—their most probable capability as determined by the staff

---

* **wargame:** A simulation, by whatever means, of a military operation involving two or more opposing forces, using rules, data, and procedures designed to depict an actual or assumed real life situation (Joint Pub 1-02). [Author's note: As defined by the Department of Defense, "war game" is an adjective and a noun. However, it is used routinely in military circles (and in this book) as a one-word verb meaning to conduct a war game.]

intelligence officer—will be used for wargaming. If there is an enemy capability that is particularly dangerous but not especially probable, that capability may be used for wargaming as well.

SELECTION OF ENEMY CAPABILITIES

The first step in analyzing courses of action is to choose which of the enemy's capabilities will be used to wargame against friendly courses of action. Other capabilities are not further considered. The choice of which enemy capabilities to consider depends on the commander's judgment. U.S. Army Field Manual 101-5, *Staff Organization and Operations,*[1] offers the following instructions:

- Analyze the enemy capabilities presented by the intelligence officer, paying particular attention to those capabilities having a high probability of adoption.
- Examine enemy capabilities to determine those that, if adopted, would produce a different effect on friendly courses of action.
- Re-examine enemy capabilities to determine which have characteristics inherent in others. For instance, between a defense in place and a delay there may be little perceived difference in their effects on friendly courses of action.
- Consider combining enemy capabilities for analysis.

The forms in tables 9.1 and 9.2 allow you to list Confederate capabilities that you, in Sherman's position, would have chosen for further analysis. In the first form, list the capability by number from chapter 6 and the rationale for your choice. In the second form, list those not chosen with the rationale for not further analyzing them. The author's choices are listed in tables 9.3 and 9.4.

WARGAMING
Background

According to FM 101-5, wargaming includes the following steps:

- Determine the combat power available on each side.
- Visualize the initial movements of friendly units.

Table 9.1 *Enemy Capabilities Chosen*

Capability	Rationale

Table 9.2 *Enemy Capabilities Not Chosen*

Capability	Rationale

TABLE 9.3 *Enemy Capabilities Chosen (Author's View)*

Capability	Rationale
D2. Reinforced defense	Most probable.
R2. Withdraw beyond the Oostanaula	Will require pursuit and river-crossing; negates most courses of action which affect primarily the position at Dalton.
A1. Penetration at Ringgold (reinforced)	Threatens Union base, particularly if the bulk of the army has maneuvered.

- Envision the effect of enemy reactions and any requirements for support, reserves, etc. after either the success or the failure of initial movements.
- Follow a similar process all the way to the final objective.

A technique often used for wargaming starts with the staff operations officer outlining the initial steps of the course of action under consideration, subject to the feasibility analyses of the logistics and communications officers. Then the staff intelligence officer outlines what he or she believes is the most likely response by the enemy, based on what he or she knows about the enemy's forces, doctrine, and even the personality of the enemy commander. His or her response is subject to feasibility analyses by the rest of the staff. The operations and intelligence officers lead the staff as they work their way through the course of action and the enemy capability until the mission is accomplished or until the course of action is shown to be infeasible. Each point at which a critical decision must be made is documented, and, where possible, both alternatives explored (see Branches and Sequels, below).

This chapter wargames in detail only one capability against one course of action as an example. At the end of this wargaming section, you have the option of listing the advantages and disadvantages of the nine Union courses of action against three broad Confederate capabilities—attack, defend, and withdraw—and then you can read the author's solution. Any wargaming needed to determine these advantages and disadvantages is left as an exercise to the reader.

TABLE 9.4 *Enemy Capabilities Not Chosen (Author's View)*

Capability	Rationale
A2. Penetration near Cleveland	Combined with A1 for consideration, as it is a lesser, related case.
A3. Penetration west of Taylor's Ridge	Too hazardous to Confederate force due to force ratios; improbable.
A4. Frontal attack	Included in A1.
A5. Single envelopment in east	Takes too long to develop; Schofield can easily counter.
A6. Infiltration north of Cleveland	Low probability. This capability takes too long to develop, allowing countermeasures.
A7. Turning movement through Alabama and Mississippi	Low probability. This capability takes too long to develop, allowing countermeasures.
A8. Infiltration to attack supply lines	Highly probable that the Confederate army will adopt this capability using its cavalry. It will affect almost all friendly courses of action in the same way, so it will not affect the choice of the proper one.
D1. Defend	Included as a lesser related case in D2.
R1. Delay on successive positions at least initially.	Indistinguishable from D2,
R3. Withdraw beyond the Etowah	Initially identical to R2.
R4. Withdraw to Kennesaw	Initially identical to R2.
R5. Withdraw to the Chattahoochee	Initially identical to R2.
R6. Withdraw to the Atlanta defenses	Initially identical to R2.
R7. Withdraw to Virginia	Initially identical to R2.

Example

For example, consider a Union turning movement across northern Alabama, course of action A9, against a Confederate reinforced defense, capability D2. The general scheme of attack would entail McPherson, with two army corps (the Army of the Tennessee), moving from the Huntsville and Stevenson areas across the Cumberland Plateau to take Rome and then on to Kingston (map 8.1). Meanwhile, Thomas and Schofield would immobilize the Confederate main body in their defenses around Dalton by conducting a supporting attack there.

The combat power available for the turning movement is about 25,000 men (30,000 if Garrard's cavalry, in Columbia, Tennessee, at the start, can be included) and almost 90,000 men are available for the supporting attack. The supporting attack would meet an entrenched defense around Dalton comprising around 50,000 men. It may not succeed against such odds, but should fix the Confederate main body in place. The turning movement would be faced with Roddey and Martin (up to 10,000 cavalry) and Polk's troops from western Alabama, another 10,000 infantry and artillery. Polk's men, although they have farther to move, could use the railroad to Blue Mountain and would almost certainly be in Rome first if they receive adequate warning from Roddey's cavalry. They would try to hold Rome—not only for the value of its factories, but also because they would stand a reasonable chance of defeating the Union attack by defending Rome's fortifications and using the cavalry to attack McPherson's supply lines.

Although only field works are in place around Rome and Polk would not have time to construct elaborate fortifications, the ruggedness of the terrain would assist his defense. The combat power available to the Union (30,000 attacking 20,000) may not be adequate without adding to the forces executing the main attack. Transferring two divisions from the closest of Thomas' corps (Hooker's XX Corps) to McPherson would give McPherson another 14,000 men and a better than two-to-one force ratio for his attack at Rome, while still allowing Thomas and Schofield a three-to-two ratio at Dalton.*

---

* In military writings it is frequent to see reference to a minimum of a three-to-one force ratio as necessary to conduct a successful attack. Although this is a useful tactical rule of thumb—other things being equal—it is totally false to extend this rule beyond the tactical arena to the operational or strategic arenas. Although it may take anywhere from three to six infantry companies to successfully attack an unsurprised, entrenched infantry company having the same weapons technology and training, two army corps with room to maneuver usually can attack one comparable army corps successfully. For units beyond mutual supporting distance (essentially line of sight in the Civil War), the three-to-one rule does not apply.

This transfer of two divisions would give each attacking commander, McPherson with the turning movement and Sherman the supporting attack, adequate strength to accomplish his missions.*

Given the augmentation of McPherson by two divisions, seven divisions of infantry and one of cavalry would have to cross the Tennessee River and then move cross-country 60 miles (100 kilometers) from the Tennessee Valley to the Coosa Valley. Gathering the forces opposite the crossing points over the Tennessee and building additional bridges would take a week—one pontoon bridge was already in place. McPherson would require at least three roads adequate for wagon traffic—one for each corps—across Sand Mountain and Lookout Mountain, and passage could take another week, because the road network barely meets this specification. Away from the roads, the slopes of the mountains are impassable to vehicles, so McPherson's maneuver options are severely constrained. Once across the mountains and having gained success at Rome, he would need a pontoon train for the Coosa or the Oostanaula River.

If Johnston does not reinforce Polk at the expense of his main body, McPherson's initial attacks should succeed in taking Rome and establishing a bridgehead across the Oostanaula River towards Kingston. Johnston must then retreat beyond the Etowah River, exposing his flank to McPherson while he retreats, or stand and fight against superior numbers with his supplies cut off. In either case there is an excellent chance to cripple the Confederate army, making further attacks towards Atlanta by the Union army easier to execute. This outcome would accomplish the Union mission.

If Johnston reinforces Polk so that he can hold Rome, Thomas and Schofield must attack against the improved odds around Dalton. If they succeed, they must pursue closely to prevent Johnston from defending the Oostanaula River. If they can force Johnston farther south, uncovering Rome, Polk must retreat and the Union army may still have a chance to cripple the Confederate army before Polk joins Johnston. On the other hand, if Johnston can hold the Union army north of the Oostanaula for one week and McPherson attacks Rome unsuccessfully,

---

* There is no evidence that Sherman planned such a transfer. He did originally plan to use Blair's two divisions (listed as reinforcements in the Union order of battle) to reinforce McPherson in order to execute this course of action, A9. See 32 *OR* 3:313. However, Blair's troops were delayed returning from furlough and could not be available by the required start time. See 32 *OR* 3:510. Hooker was a senior general—he had commanded the Army of the Potomac at Chancellorsville—and might well have objected to serving under the just-promoted McPherson or to having his divisions transferred.

McPherson will run low on supplies and must retreat north towards Chattanooga. Remember, McPherson must start his retreat when he still has enough supplies to reach Chattanooga. He cannot return across the mountains (where there is little or no forage available) without risking destruction. Foraging and carried supplies will not sustain McPherson much beyond three weeks in the field unless he can rejoin the rest of the army and draw forage from them. If the Confederates reinforce at Rome, the mission cannot be accomplished unless Thomas and Schofield can force Johnston from Dalton and from the Oostanaula River.

Branches and Sequels

The discussion in the previous section is an example of examining what the modern military calls "branches and sequels." A branch is a point in time when a decision must be taken between two or more alternatives, or a point when the enemy can react in two or more distinct ways. A sequel is a subsequent operation that follows a decision or the completion of an action or phase.

Figure 9.1 illustrates the branches and sequels encountered in examining Union course of action A9, assuming that McPherson is reinforced by two divisions from Thomas's army. In this flow chart, diamonds indicate branches and rectangles indicate sequels. All the branches here are yes/no questions, but this will not always be true—some questions can be answered in multiple ways and may result in several branches, not just two.

The first branch point is Johnston's decision as to whether to reinforce Polk at the expense of Johnston's army around Dalton. If he does, McPherson needs to demonstrate heavily as if he were going to attack Rome, but not sacrifice his soldiers. Thomas and Schofield must attack to break Johnston's weakened position at Dalton. On the other hand, if Johnston does not reinforce Polk, McPherson must conduct an all-out attack, perhaps trying to achieve tactical surprise and not using the obvious approach that he would have if he were only making a demonstration.

Thus, one of the key intelligence indicators Sherman must look for is whether Johnston significantly reinforces Polk. Modern commanders would call this a "commander's critical intelligence requirement." Receiving this intelligence would allow Sherman to decide which should be the main attack, Thomas and Schofield or McPherson. McPherson must plan for success by having a pontoon train ready for crossing the Coosa-Etowah-Oostanaula Rivers, and having a plan to seize the

FIGURE 9.1 *Branches and Sequels*

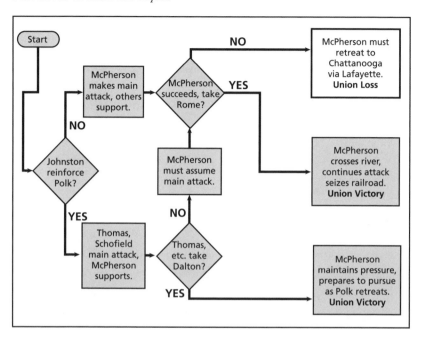

Western and Atlantic Railroad near Kingston. He must also plan for a retreat through LaFayette to Chattanooga if both attacks fail.

Conclusions about the Example

The Union course of action A9 has both advantages and disadvantages when wargamed against the Confederate reinforced defense D2. Such an attack avoids placing the main effort against the strongest part of the Confederate defenses. The attack stresses Confederate command and control by attacking simultaneously at two points. A McPherson victory could lead to decisive results for the campaign overall. On the other hand, the terrain does not favor an approach across Sand and Lookout mountains. A defeat or even a stalemate—a common result of Civil War battles—would leave a portion of the Union army at risk. The plan risks much but has the promise of overwhelming success.

ADVANTAGES AND DISADVANTAGES

Upon completion of wargaming selected enemy capabilities against proposed courses of action, the commander and staff should have a feeling for how each course of action plays against enemy capabilities. FM 101-5 lists some of the information that might be developed:

- Requirements for readjustment of initial dispositions . . . [and] composition of main and supporting attack forces,
- Probable enemy reactions,
- Probable critical areas and incidents and how success is to be achieved in each case,
- Attrition of friendly and enemy forces,
- Location and composition of the reserve and its possible employment,
- Actions required in the objective area, and
- Advantages and disadvantages of each course of action.[2]

You can wargame other courses of action against enemy capabilities. A formal branches and sequels chart is not necessary but would be valuable. The end result of such wargaming should be a list of advantages and disadvantages associated with each combination. These then can be listed in table 9.5, which shows the author's nine Union attack options and three Confederate capabilities (attack, defend, and retrograde corresponding to A1, D2, and R2), but changes can be made as necessary.

TABLE 9.5 *Union Advantages and Disadvantages*

Union Course	Confederate Capabilities		
of Action	Attack	Defend	Withdraw
A1. Frontal Attack (attack southeast through railroad pass and south from Cleveland toward Dalton)			
A2. Penetrate Buzzard's Roost (direct attack through railroad pass)			

continued

TABLE 9.5 *Union Advantages and Disadvantages, continued*

Union Course of Action	Confederate Capabilities		
	Attack	Defend	Withdraw
A3. Penetration south from Red Clay (south of Cleveland)			
A4. Single envelopment from east of Red Clay			
A5. Envelopment at Dug's Gap (through Rocky Face south of the railroad gap)			
A6. Double envelopment (A4 and A5)			
A7. Shallow turning movement through Snake Creek Gap			
A8. Deep turning movement west of Taylor's Ridge to Rome			
A9. Turning movement across north Alabama to Rome			

Table 9.6 offers the author's solution. This listing of advantages and disadvantages will be used when comparing the various friendly courses of action in order to make a decision.

TABLE 9.6 *Union Advantages and Disadvantages (Author's View)*

Union Course of Action	Confederate Capabilities		
	Attack	Defend	Withdraw
A1. Frontal attack	• Terrain and logistics favorable • Probable heavy losses to enemy • Good probability of mission accomplishment • Difficult to coordinate	• Simple plan • Logistics easy • Hits main defense • Probable heavy losses • Terrain barrier • Low probability of mission accomplishment	• Simple plan • Logistics easy • Terrain favorable • Little effect on enemy army
A2. Penetrate Buzzard's Roost	• Terrain and logistics favorable • Probable heavy losses to enemy • Difficult to coordinate • Low probability of mission accomplishment	• Simple plan • Logistics easy • Hits main defense • Terrain barrier • Inadequate maneuver space • Probable heavy losses • Low probability of mission accomplishment	• Simple plan • Logistics easy • Terrain favorable • Little effect on enemy army
A3. Penetrate north of Dalton	• Terrain and logistics favorable • Probable heavy losses to enemy • Good probability of success • Difficult to coordinate of mission accomplishment	• Simple plan • Logistics easy • Terrain favorable • Risks heavy casualties • Exposes supply lines slightly • Low probability	• Simple plan • Logistics easy • Terrain favorable • Little effect on enemy army

continued

TABLE 9.6 *Union Advantages and Disadvantages (Author's View), continued*

Union Course of Action	Confederate Capabilities		
	Attack	Defend	Withdraw
A4. Envelopment northeast of Dalton	• Terrain and logistics favorable • Probable heavy losses to enemy • Possibility of enemy local success • Difficult to coordinate	• Terrain favorable • Logistics easy • Avoids main defense • Good chance of success • Exposes supply lines • Coordination difficult	• Logistics easy • Terrain favorable • Minor effect on enemy army
A5. Envelopment at Dug's Gap	• Terrain and logistics favorable • Probable enemy heavy losses • Difficult to coordinate • Low probability of mission accomplishment	• Simple plan • Logistics easy • Inadequate maneuver space/bad terrain • Probable heavy losses • Low probability of mission accomplishment	• Simple plan • Logistics easy • Minor effect on enemy army
A6. Double envelopment (A4 and A5)	• Terrain and logistics favorable • Probable enemy heavy losses • Possibility of enemy local success • Difficult to coordinate	• Logistics easy • Avoids main defense • Bad terrain • Complex plan • Possible heavy losses • Coordination very difficult	• Logistics easy • Minor effect on enemy army
A7. Turning movement through Snake Creek Gap	• Terrain and logistics favorable • Probable heavy losses to enemy • Very difficult to coordinate • Possibility of enemy success	• Avoids main defense • Logistics easy • Good probability of mission accomplishment • Attack can be bottled in gap • Coordination difficult	• Can gain surprise • Logistics easy • Could trap a major part of the enemy army • Gap easy to block

continued

TABLE 9.6 *Union Advantages and Disadvantages (Author's View), continued*

Union Course of Action	Confederate Capabilities		
	Attack	Defend	Withdraw
A8. Turning movement through LaFayette	• Terrain favorable • Success would be decisive • McPherson too far to help main army • Coordination very difficult • Enemy success could imperil McPherson	• Avoids main defense • Good probability of mission accomplishment • Logistics difficult • Coordination very difficult	• Can gain surprise • Could trap a major part of the enemy army • May take too long to be effective
A9. Turning movement across north Alabama	• Terrain favorable • Success would be decisive • McPherson too far to help main army • Coordination very difficult • Enemy success could imperil McPherson	• Avoids main defense • Stresses enemy command • Possible decisive results • Terrain/logistics unfavorable • Coordination very difficult	• Can gain surprise • Could trap a major part of the enemy army • May take too long to be effective

Again, the advantages and disadvantages given here are just one opinion. A modern staff, if afforded the luxury of time, would argue over almost every word in the list.

END-OF-CHAPTER NOTES

1. Field Manual 101-5, *Staff Organization and Operations* (Washington, D.C.: Department of the Army, 1984), p. E-5.
2. FM 101-5, p. E-7.

CHAPTER 10

Comparison of
Courses of Action

ESTIMATE OF THE SITUATION

I. MISSION
II. THE SITUATION AND COURSES OF ACTION
III. ANALYSIS OF OPPOSING COURSES OF ACTION
IV. COMPARISON OF OWN COURSES OF ACTION
V. DECISION

In order to make a decision, the commander must compare the available courses of action. Usually a commander compares the advantages and disadvantages of each course of action, although some advantages may not be very significant compared to others. Greater weight is usually given to advantages and disadvantages arising from more probable enemy capabilities, although due regard is given to any capability that may not seem probable but that would be very dangerous if adopted by the enemy. Remember that the most probable Confederate course of action is to defend; the next most probable, to withdraw. The least probable is for a Confederate attack—except raiding of supply lines, which can be expected.

Two techniques for comparing courses of action are recommended in FM 101-5, *Staff Organization and Operations*. The first consists of listing the significant advantages and disadvantages of each course of action and discussing each. It is used when time is short or choices clear-cut.

The second technique—more difficult, yet arguably more useful—is a two-stage process. The commander decides on factors such as enemy locations, terrain, logistics, probability of mission accomplishment, and so on, that are the most significant given the specific situation. A concrete list of factors usable in every situation cannot be given because situations differ, so the factors that are of the greatest significance differ also. Once these significant factors are chosen, the advantages and disadvantages of each course of action are listed in a decision table under the appropriate factors. The commander makes a judgment as to which courses of action are favored by a particular factor, and, after considering all factors, draws a conclusion as to the best course of action to follow.

EXAMPLE DECISION TABLE

An example of a simple decision table is given in table 10.1, taken directly from FM 101-5.[1]

TABLE 10.1 *Sample Decision Table*

	Significant Factors			
Course of Action	**Dispositions**	**Weather/ Terrain**	**Supporting Attack**	**Obstacles**
Course of Action 1	Avoids main enemy strength.	Not the best avenue of approach to division objective.	Relies heavily on success of supporting attack.	Encounters a limited number of artificial obstacles.
Course of Action 2	Hits main enemy strength.	Best of the avenues of approach to division objective being considered. Secures dominant terrain.	Not as dependent on success of supporting attack.	Encounters a large number of artificial obstacles.
Favors	Course of action 1 over course of action 2.	Course of action 2 over course of action 1.	Course of action 2 over course of action 1.	Course of action 1 over course of action 2.

TABLE 10.2 *Possible Significant Factors*

Principles of War	Dynamics of Combat Power	Combat Functions Combat Functions	Other
Objective	Maneuver	Intelligence	Sustainment
Offensive	Firepower	Maneuver	Terrain
Mass	Protection	Fire Support	Weather
Economy of Force	Leadership	Air Defense	Combined
Maneuver		Mobility and	Arms
Unity of Command		Survivability	Deception
Security		Logistics	Flexibility
Surprise		Battle Command	Audacity
Simplicity			

SIGNIFICANT FACTORS

To apply the two-stage process, the commander must first choose the factors appropriate to the situation. The choice should be based on the commander's restated mission and understanding of the situation based on those portions of the estimate already completed. Too many factors will confuse the analysis, but the use of too few will prevent a clear decision. Possible factors that could be considered—all taken from various lists in FM 100-5—are listed in table 10.2 and defined in the glossary.[2] Other important factors may be considered in particular situations.

List the factors that you consider significant in the following table:

The author chose eight factors from table 10.2, then combined several to yield five columns for the decision table: terrain and maneuver, sustainment, unity of command and simplicity, firepower and protection, and objective. These are listed approximately in increasing order of importance, but sometimes numerical weights can be assigned to each factor. The rationale for choosing these factors over other entries comes from an analysis of the mission and table 9.6, which lists advantages and disadvantages of each course of action in the context of the situation. The chosen factors are used repeatedly to describe course of action advantages and disadvantages.

TABLE 10.3 *Decision Table*

Significant Factors					
Course of Action	Terrain/ Maneuver	Sustainment	Unity of Command/ Simplicity	Firepower/ Protection	Objective/ Mission Accomplishment
A1.					
A2.					
A3.					
A4.					
A5.					
A6.					
A7.					
A8.					
A9.					
Favors					

Conclusion:

_____

_____

_____

_____

_____

_____

_____

_____

DECISION TABLES

You are invited to fill in table 10.3, the decision table, based on table 9.6 and your own judgment. The author's factors are filled in across the top, but you may want to use your own instead. After finishing the table, state a conclusion as to the best course of action. If you are working in a group, be prepared to defend the conclusion! Table 10.4 shows the author's solution.

CONCLUSION

The choice must be made from among A4, A6, A7, A8, and A9, because they all offer a good probability of success—see the last, most important column (Objective/Mission Accomplishment). A9 is the best in terms of firepower and protection but worst for sustainment, unity of command, and simplicity. It can be eliminated on that basis. A6 also is very complex and difficult to command and not well supported by the terrain, and A8 is complex and difficult to sustain. A4 and A7 appear somewhat better. Referring to table 9.6, A4 is a little better—based on maneuver space— than A7, given a Confederate defense or attack, and A7 looks a little better if the Confederates withdraw.

TABLE 10.4 *Decision Table (Author's View)*

Significant Factors

Course of Action	Terrain/ Maneuver	Sustainment	Unity of Command/ Simplicity	Firepower/ Protection	Objective/ Mission Accom- plishment
A1. Frontal	Somewhat unfavorable	Very favorable	Very favorable	Very unfavorable	Small chance
A2. Penetrate	Very unfavorable	Very favorable	Very favorable	Very unfavorable	Very small chance
A3. Penetrate north of Dalton	Somewhat favorable	Favorable	Favorable	Somewhat unfavorable	Small chance
A4. Envelop North	Favorable	Somewhat favorable	Somewhat unfavorable	Favorable	Good chance
A5. Envelop South	Very unfavorable	Very favorable	Favorable	Unfavorable	Very small chance
A6. Double envelop	Unfavorable	Favorable	Unfavorable	Unfavorable	Good chance
A7. Turning movement through Snake Creek Gap	Somewhat favorable	Favorable	Somewhat unfavorable	Favorable	Good chance
A8. Turn LaFayette	Favorable	Unfavorable	Unfavorable	Favorable	Good chance

continued

TABLE 10.4 *Decision Table (Author's View), continued*

Significant Factors

Course of Action	Terrain/ Maneuver	Sustainment	Unity of Command/ Simplicity	Firepower/ Protection	Objective/ Mission Accomplishment
A9. Turn through North Alabama	Unfavorable	Very unfavorable	Very unfavorable	Very favorable	Good chance
Favors	A4, A8 best; A3, A7 second best; A2, A5 worst	A1, A2, A5 best; A9 worst; A8 second worst	A1, A2 best; A3, A5 second best; A9 worst; A6, A8 second worst	A9 best; A4, A7, A8 second best; A1, A2 worst	A4, A6, A7, A8, A9 best; A2, A5 worst

END-OF-CHAPTER NOTES

1. FM 101-5, E-9.
2. FM 101-5, various tables and lists.

CHAPTER 11

Decision and Concept of the Operation

ESTIMATE OF THE SITUATION

I. MISSION
II. THE SITUATION AND COURSES OF ACTION
III. ANALYSIS OF OPPOSING COURSES OF ACTION
IV. COMPARISON OF OWN COURSES OF ACTION
V. DECISION

The bottom line—the result of all the information gathered and analysis performed earlier—is the decision. Make your decision based on the conclusions from table 10.3 (or table 10.4, if you are just following the author's analysis).

Course of Action Chosen	Rationale

The author chose A4, to envelop the Confederate left flank northeast of Dalton. That decision was based on the prediction that the Confederate Army would choose to defend, and that in course of action A4 the various components of the Union Army would be closer together for mutual support, should the need arise.

Sherman's decision was A7. He apparently decided that the chance of greater payoff—the possibility that the Confederates might not close Snake Creek Gap in time—was worth the risk. As you shall see, he was right.

CONCEPT OF THE OPERATION

The commander's decision must translate the chosen course of action into a clear statement of what will be done, when, where the action will take place, how, who will play the various parts, and why. The commander relays this decision to subordinates as his or her "concept of the operation," a description of how the commander visualizes the operation from start to finish. The commander's concept should contain enough detail so that, if necessary, subordinates can accomplish the mission without further instructions. FM 101-5, *Staff Organization and Operations*, contains a partial list of what should be included in the commander's concept.[1] An extract of those items from the list that are particularly relevant to Sherman's decision is:

- How the units are organized (task organization). This entry lists the major subdivisions of the army and the composition of those major subdivisions.
- Employment of the major maneuver elements—how they are to move.
- Command and control arrangements (command relationships and command post locations).
- Contingency plans (sequels or "what ifs").
- Liaison/coordination—how units maintain contact.

READER'S CONCEPT OF THE OPERATION

The blanks on the next page offer you a chance to state your own concept of the operation. Usually the mission is restated before the concept is outlined, but chapter 5 contains the mission restatement, which is not reproduced here here. Map 11.1 is provided for reference.

Map 11.1 *Details of Dalton Area*

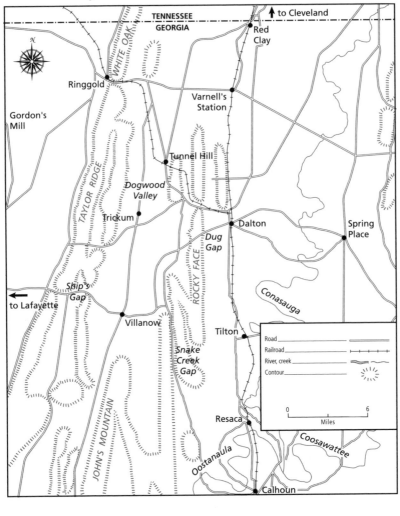

Task organization	
Employment of major maneuver elements	
Command and control arrangements	
Contingency plans	
Liaison/ Coordination	

AUTHOR'S CONCEPT OF THE OPERATION

The following tables display the author's solution to a concept of operation for course of action A4, a single envelopment of the Confederate right flank northeast of Dalton. Map 11.2, a reprint of map 11.1 with the addition of proposed Union positions, shows the author's decision graphically.

MAP 11.2 *Author's Attack Plan (A4)*

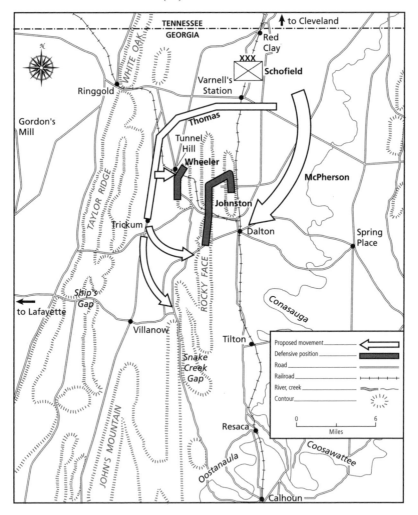

Task organization	Army of the Cumberland (3 corps, 9 infantry divisions) with the Cavalry Corps (2 divisions) initially attached— **THOMAS**
	Army of the Tennessee (2 corps, 5 infantry divisions)— **MCPHERSON**
	Army of the Ohio (1 corps, 3 infantry divisions)— **SCHOFIELD**
Employment of major maneuver elements	The Army of the Cumberland will move from its present positions to establish an arc of infantry positions from one mile east of Varnell's Station on the Red Clay–Dalton Road to Trickum. The Confederate position at Tunnel Hill— lightly held—will be taken on Saturday, 7 May. At dawn on 8 May, elements of the army not to exceed one corps will demonstrate against Dug Gap and Snake Creek Gap to create a diversion but will not attack unless there is a high probability of success. If there is little resistance, seize the gap(s) and fortify your position, informing headquarters immediately of a success. Other units will drive in the enemy skirmishers but will not conduct a major attack. With its presence and with the balance of the cavalry, the Army of the Cumberland will screen the movement of the Army of the Tennessee into its attack position behind the far left and will attempt to deceive the enemy as to the location of the main effort. The cavalry will concentrate its reconnaissance on the army's left (enemy's right) flank and be prepared to pass to McPherson's control upon his arrival.
	The Army of the Tennessee under McPherson will move by rail to Red Clay, then deploy along the Dalton Road behind the cover of the cavalry. Upon reaching that position, not later than dawn on 8 May, McPherson will receive control from Thomas of the reinforced cavalry division there and reconnoiter the enemy's right flank. Not before 8 AM or later than 10 AM, McPherson will attack this flank at a point of his choosing so as to seize Dalton and cut off the enemy forces north and west of the town.
	The Army of the Ohio will move from Cleveland south to Red Clay after the Army of the Tennessee has cleared the station. They will be the army group reserve, preparing to reinforce a successful attack or to conduct a pursuit to and beyond the Oostanaula.

continued

Command and control	The commander-in-chief will be at Ringgold until the afternoon of 7 May, then move to Varnell's Station.
Contingency plans	If the enemy army appears to be retreating at any time, the corps or army commander first receiving notice will immediately start a pursuit while notifying higher commanders. Care should be taken to avoid firing into friendly troops, as those pursuing could converge around Dalton. If the enemy attacks, units are to hold their present ground and the maneuver will continue, as any forward movement of the enemy's forces would place them even farther from their lines of retreat. In extremis, units of the Army of the Cumberland west of Rocky Face can retreat as far back as Taylor's Ridge, which must be held. The line Ringgold–Varnell's Station must be held to protect the trains. If McPherson cannot take Dalton, he will turn over his forward positions to Thomas and attempt to bypass enemy defenses by their eastern flank, continuing the attack into Dalton. If his troops are too tired to continue, he will pass the cavalry to Schofield, who will move up with his army and continue the attack around the east flank of the Confederate Army. In this case, the southernmost (right) corps of Thomas' army will be withdrawn from their deception operation and become army group reserve. If the enemy does not defend Dug or Snake Creek gaps and the attack north of Dalton bogs down, on order Thomas will move southwest of Rocky Face Ridge to exploit that opening. If this occurs, Schofield should be prepared to fill in Thomas's positions and McPherson should be prepared to pull one corps out of his line to reconstitute the reserve.
Liaison/ coordination	Thomas will maintain contact with McPherson at all times. As McPherson drives forward, Thomas will move his units to maintain contact. Commanders will maintain contact with units on either side.

SHERMAN'S CONCEPT OF THE OPERATION

Although there is no evidence that Sherman held an operations briefing such as that often conducted by modern commanders, he met with each subordinate commander in turn. Additionally, he conducted an extensive correspondence with these subordinates, from which it is possible to extract the information normally included in the commander's concept. The two pieces of correspondence shown here are representative. Remember, Sherman adopted course of action A7, a turning movement through Snake Creek Gap to Resaca.

Map 11.3 *Sherman's Actual Plan of Attack*

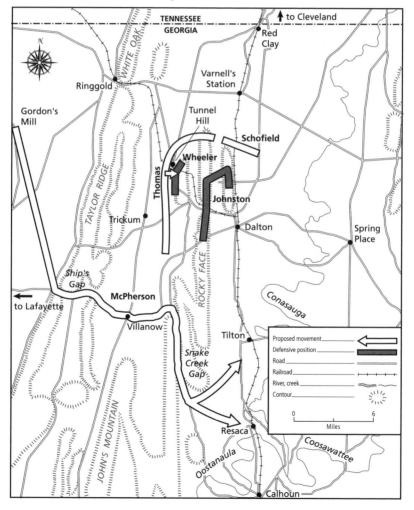

SPECIAL   HDQRS. MIL. DIV. OF THE
ORDERS NO. 35   MISSISSIPPI
Nashville, Tenn., April 25, 1864

I. The armies now on the line of the Tennessee for the purpose of war will constitute one army, under the personal direction of the major-general commanding the division[2] . . .

II. The effective Army of the Cumberland will be the center, that of the Ohio the left wing, and that of the Tennessee the right wing. . . . The commander-in-chief will be habitually with the center. . . .

III. General Stoneman, under Major-General Schofield, will command the cavalry of the left, and General Gerrard . . . is temporarily attached to the right, and will receive orders from Major-General McPherson. . . . Major-General Thomas will organize out of his remaining cavalry force a division to act on his front. . . .

        By order of Maj. Gen. W. T. Sherman:
            R. M. SAWYER,
           Assistant Adjutant-General.[3]

HDQRS. MIL. DIV. OF THE MISSISSIPPI,
In the Field, Ringgold, Ga., May 5, 1864

Maj. Gen. G. H. THOMAS,
Commanding Army of the Cumberland:

SIR: The position of our troops to-morrow night, the 6th instant, will be, Schofield at Red Clay, you at Ringgold, and McPherson at Gordons Mills. The plan of action will be: you move in force on Tunnel Hill, secure it and threaten Dalton in front, but not to attack its defenses until further orders, unless the enemy assume the offensive against either of our wings, when all must attack directly in front toward the enemy's main army and not without

continued

orders detach to the relief of the threatened wing. At the time you move against Tunnel Hill McPherson will move to Ship's Gap and Villanow, and secure possession of Snake Creek Gap, from which he will operate vigorously against the enemy's flank or line of communication between Tilton Station and Resaca. I want you, with cavalry or infantry, to fill well up Dogwood Valley, and communicate with McPherson at Villanow. Trains likely to embarrass our movements should not be taken east of Taylor's Ridge, till we have observed the effect of these first movements. I expect to be all ready to move on Saturday, and wish you to make all preparations accordingly.

I am, &c.,

W. T. SHERMAN,
Major-General, Commanding.[4]

The following paragraphs show Sherman's concept of the operation by taking language from the letters and placing it in the format given earlier. Map 11.3 gives all the locations cited and graphically shows Sherman's actual plan. Note that although Sherman did not use a definite format, he did include all the elements of a concept of the operation in his orders and letters to his subordinates.

Task organization	The armies now on the line of the Tennessee for the purpose of war will constitute one army. Major General Thomas will organize . . . a [cavalry] division to act on his front.
Employment of major maneuver elements	The effective Army of the Cumberland will be the center, that of the Ohio the left wing, and that of the Tennessee the right wing. The plan of action will be: you [Thomas] move in force on Tunnel Hill, secure it and threaten Dalton in front, but not to attack its defenses until further orders. At the time you [Thomas] move against Tunnel Hill, McPherson will move to Ship's Gap and Villanow, and secure possession of Snake Creek Gap, from which he will operate vigorously against the enemy's flank or line of communication between Tilton Station and Resaca. Trains likely to embarrass our movements should not be

continued

	taken east of Taylor's Ridge, till we have observed the effect of these first movements. I expect to be all ready to move on Saturday, and wish you to make all preparations accordingly.
Command and control arrangements	The armies . . . will constitute one army, under the personal direction of the major-general commanding the division. The commander-in-chief will be habitually with the center. General Stoneman, under Major General Schofield, will command the cavalry of the left, and General Garrard . . . will receive orders from Major General McPherson.
Contingency plans	. . . not to attack its defenses [Rocky Face and Buzzard's Roost] until further orders, unless the enemy assume the offensive against either of our wings, when all must attack directly in front toward the enemy's main army and not without orders detach to the relief of the threatened wing.
Liaison/ coordination	The position of our troops to-morrow night, the 6th instant, will be, Schofield at Red Clay, you [Thomas] at Ringgold, and McPherson at Gordon's Mills. I want you, with cavalry or infantry, to fill well up Dogwood Valley, and communicate with McPherson at Villanow.

END-OF-CHAPTER NOTES

1.   FM 101-5, 5-10.
2.   "Division" here means the Military Division of Mississippi, not a unit such as a division of infantry.
3.   32 *OR* 3:496.
4.   38 *OR* 4:35.

Part Three
The Rest
of the Story

CHAPTER 12

Ground Truth

C hapter 6 gives Sherman's appreciation of the strength, locations, and intentions of the Confederate Army. This chapter
examines the actual Confederate political and command environment, the true strengths and locations of the Confederate Army, and
Johnston's intentions.

THE CONFEDERATE POLITICAL AND COMMAND ENVIRONMENT

The political climate in the Confederacy during early 1864 was in many
ways worse than that in the Union. Although Confederate President
Jefferson Davis did not face elections—he had been elected to a single
term that was to end in 1868—there was significant opposition to him
personally in the Confederate Congress. The South had lost many men
and much territory following Davis's military policies. Some areas nominally under government control were actually in an anarchic state, overrun by deserters and draft dodgers.

The president directly controlled the appointment of almost all officers.
He and General Johnston, Sherman's opponent, had had a long-standing
feud, dating back at least to the period when Davis was the United States
Secretary of War in 1855.[1] This acrimony had been exacerbated by fric-
tion between the two during the Peninsula Campaign in Virginia in 1862,
based on Johnston's unwillingness to share his plans with Davis. There had
been even more friction during the Vicksburg campaign. Davis blamed
Johnston for the loss of Vicksburg and its army, even though Lieutenant
General John C. Pemberton, in charge of Vicksburg, had disobeyed
Johnston's orders during the campaign. This disobedience had resulted in
the loss of Pemberton's army along with Vicksburg itself. Davis removed
Johnston after Vicksburg, but was later forced by the Confederate Congress to appoint him commander of the Army of Tennessee. This occurred
after General Braxton Bragg, the former commander, failed to maintain
the siege of Chattanooga and lost control of his army, routed by Grant's

attack in November 1864. In Davis's mind, all other alternatives had been exhausted, so Johnston was reappointed. Davis hated and distrusted Johnston, and Johnston reciprocated.

Upon Bragg's removal from the command of the Army of Tennessee, Davis appointed Bragg as his chief of staff. Military communications went through Bragg and he participated in all planning sessions. Politically he was a poor choice, because neither the Confederate Congress nor the army had any confidence in Bragg. Bragg distrusted most of the officers of the Army of Tennessee because they had conspired to have him removed for incompetence. He had little interest in Johnston's succeeding where he had failed, and he was totally dependent on Davis as his only patron and political sponsor. However, Bragg and Johnston seemed to get along well and Johnston depended on Bragg to present accurate military judgments to Davis.

During the campaign, Johnston had four principal subordinates: Lieutenant General William J. Hardee, Lieutenant General John B. Hood, Lieutenant General Leonidas Polk, and Major General Joseph Wheeler. Photos 6.4 through 6.7 are of these generals.

Hardee, the temporary commander of the army after Bragg's relief, had been offered permanent command of the army before Johnston, but had turned it down, citing personal reasons. He was a capable and highly respected officer and the author of the standard drill text used by both sides, *Rifle and Light Infantry Tactics*. His complaints had helped engineer Bragg's removal.

Hood had made a name for himself as a division commander under General Lee, but had no real experience in corps command. Lee's letter to Davis when Davis proposed replacing Johnston with Hood shows best what the informed opinion of Hood was:

> Hood is a bold fighter. I am doubtful as to the other qualities necessary . . . Hood is very industrious on the battlefield, careless off, and I have had no opportunity of judging his action, when the whole responsibility rested upon him. I have a high opinion of his gallantry, earnestness, and zeal.[2]

Hood was a favorite of Davis and wrote Davis personal letters critical of Johnston, although Johnston was not aware of this at the time and took

Hood into his confidence more than he did any other subordinate commander.

Polk was a respected but not very capable officer, and at the opening of the campaign had an independent command in western Alabama and Mississippi. He was a West Point graduate, as were all Johnston's principal subordinates and almost everyone appointed to high rank by Jefferson Davis (a West Pointer himself), but he had quit the Army upon graduation, joined the Episcopal ministry, and eventually became a bishop. He corresponded directly with Davis, his friend, and also had helped engineer Bragg's removal.

Bragg had promoted Wheeler to head the Army of Tennessee's cavalry. Wheeler was competent and enthusiastic but lacked maturity and experience at higher command. He was not thorough in performing the dull work of gathering intelligence and protecting the army. Johnston depended upon him perhaps too much for information about the terrain and the enemy.

Johnston faced a difficult task. As he surveyed his army in the spring of 1864, he could see weaknesses (primarily in being greatly outnumbered by Sherman in soldiers and healthy animals) and strengths (in the terrain and in the experience of his soldiers).

CONFEDERATE COMBAT POWER
Location and Dispositions
Map 12.1 shows the locations of the army on 30 April 1864.

Strength and Composition
Table 12.1 records the total number of men present (recorded as aggregate present) in Johnston's army—almost 64,000. This number includes sick personnel, cavalrymen without horses, and other personnel not militarily effective. The number of effectives reported (which excluded officers and the ineffective personnel listed previously) was almost 44,000. The report was the official return of Johnston's Army, dated 30 April 1864. It is worth comparing the following information with that in chapter 6. Sherman's information about the Confederate Army, detailed there, was very accurate.

Hardee's Corps had Cheatham's Division (5,696 soldiers), Cleburne's Division (6,909), Walker's Division (6,916), and Bate's Division (4,675),

Map 12.1 *Actual Locations of Johnston's Army*

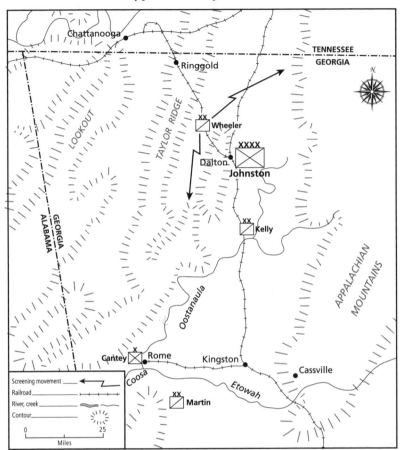

plus headquarters and artillery. Hood had Hindman's Division (7,614), Stevenson's Division (8,060), and Stewart's Division (7,373), plus headquarters and artillery. Brigadier General James Cantey's Brigade, at Rome and not yet joined, additionally had about 400 men of the 37th Mississippi Infantry Regiment en route and not counted in the table.

The Cavalry Corps under Wheeler had Martin's Division near Rome (2,538), Brigadier General John H. Kelly's Division at Resaca (2,749), and part of Brigadier General William Y. C. Hume's Division in the rear "recruiting horses." The balance of Hume's Division (total division strength 2,618), Colonel J. Warren Grigsby's Brigade (1,115), and Colonel Moses W. Hannon's Brigade (784), plus staff and some artillery was forward screening the front and flanks of the army.

TABLE 12.1 *Composition and Strength of the Confederate Army*

Unit	Commander	Present for Duty	Cannon	Source
Headquarters		208	—	38 *OR* 3:865
Hardee's Corps	Hardee	25,792	48	38 *OR* 3:866
Hood's Corps	Hood	24,369	36	38 *OR* 3:866
Cantey's Brigade	Cantey	1,860	6	38 *OR* 3:866
Cavalry Corps	Wheeler	10,058	18	38 *OR* 3:866
Artillery Reserve	Hallonquist	1,048	36	38 *OR* 3:866
Engineer troops	Presstman	477	—	38 *OR* 3:865
TOTAL	Johnston	63,812	144	

Reinforcements

Potential reinforcements for Johnston as of 30 April 1864 included:

- Polk's Corps (called the Army of Mississippi in the returns dated 30 April 1864):
  — Loring's Division (5,126 men and 18 cannon present) at Montevallo, Alabama
  — French's Division (2,492 men and 6 cannon present) at Tuscaloosa, Alabama
  — Brigadier General Claudius W. Sears' Brigade of French's Division (1,921 men) at Selma en route to Tuscaloosa, Alabama
- S. D. Lee's cavalry (about 10,000 men total):
  — Two brigades of Brigadier General William H. Jackson's Division at Tuscaloosa, Alabama
  — Brigadier General Samuel W. Ferguson's brigade at Elyton, Alabama (now Birmingham)
  — Brigadier General William Wirt Adam's brigade at Yazoo City, Mississippi
  — One brigade near Baton Rouge, Louisiana (Scott?)
  — One brigade of Brigadier General James R. Chalmer's Division near Grenada, Mississippi, and Brigadier General Abraham Buford's Division (about 1,500 men[3]) under Major General Forrest's personal command, raiding in Jackson, Tennessee, on 28 April and expected to return to Tupelo, Mississippi, by 6 May[4]
  — Roddey's cavalry in north Alabama, under Lee's command but not included in his count, probably numbered around 2,000[5]

MAP 12.2 *Positions of Possible Reinforcements*

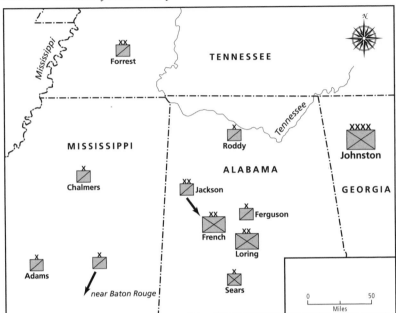

Other, smaller forces from the Atlantic and Gulf Coasts were eventually ordered to reinforce Johnston as well. Map 12.2 shows the location of these possible reinforcements.

Logistics

One observer of a grand review held on 19 April wrote, "The army presented itself in the best condition that I have ever witnessed."[6] Weapons and ammunition were present in adequate numbers, but other equipment such as knapsacks, bayonets, and small-arm implements were short.[7] More important was that the army was short at least 1,000 wagons and some unspecified number of artillery horses.[8] In March a thorough inspection of the artillery of the army showed 42 artillery pieces to be too obsolete for proper usage and a shortage of 500 horses in the artillery alone.[9] As with all Confederate armies, supplies and equipment were present but shortages were manifest.

Time and Space Factors

The main Confederate Army was in close proximity to Union positions and could attack with little warning, measured in hours. However, an attack had little prospect of success due to the disparity in strengths between the armies. As stated in chapter 6, the army could redeploy against Union positions in north Alabama by either train—via Mobile, Alabama, and Tupelo, Mississippi—or road, but such a movement would take several weeks and would leave Atlanta uncovered. The army could move by train to Virginia to reinforce General Lee, but that move would also take several weeks and would leave the entire center of the Confederacy uncovered.

Polk's corps (the Army of Mississippi), using a combination of marching and railroads, could reinforce Johnston, closing in about two weeks, but President Davis did not desire this because the supplies, especially foodstuffs, in the area of eastern Mississippi and western Alabama were so valuable.[10] When Polk did move to reinforce Johnston, he left S. D. Lee's cavalry to protect Mississippi with permission to conduct raids if Union pressure allowed Lee (or, more to the point, Forrest) to do so.

Combat Efficiency

Johnston's officers and his army were veteran soldiers. Although some soldiers deserted and others had low morale, the majority appears to have had full confidence in their general and their army. At the beginning of the campaign, they were as efficient as the Army of Tennessee had ever been or would ever be. They would prove to be formidable foes.

JOHNSTON'S INTENTIONS

General Johnston received his initial instructions by letter directly from President Davis and from Secretary of War James A. Seddon, and his routine instructions came through General Bragg. The instructions that Johnston received were clear, but—with the exception of one impractical plan—not detailed. Johnston was properly allowed wide latitude in the performance of his mission. Excerpts from his instructions are shown next. Although these instructions date from December 1863, subsequent messages did not materially modify them.

WAR DEPARTMENT, C. S. A.,
Richmond, Va., December 18, 1863.

General JOSEPH E. JOHNSTON:

GENERAL: . . .

It is desired that your early and vigorous efforts be directed to restoring the discipline, confidence, and prestige of the army and to increasing its numbers, and that at the same time you leave no means unspared to restore and supply its deficiencies in ordnance, numbers, and transportation. . . .

The movements of the enemy give no present indications of a purpose to attack your army, and it is probable that they may mean to strengthen themselves in the occupation of the portions of Tennessee they have overrun. It is not desirable they should be allowed to do so with impunity, and as soon as the condition of your forces will allow it is hoped you will be able to assume the offensive.

. . . Should the enemy venture to separate his army or send off detachments on different expeditions, it is hoped you may be able early to strike them with effect. . . . [Y]our own experience and judgment are relied on to form and act on your own plans. . . . [O]ther imperative claims on the Department must confine you almost exclusively to the resources of your present department and such general aids as it may be in the power of General Polk to render . . .

Very truly, yours,
JAMES A. SEDDON,
SECRETARY OF WAR.[11]

EXECUTIVE DEPARTMENT,
Richmond, December 23, 1863.

General J. E. JOHNSTON,
Commanding, &c., Dalton, Ga.:

GENERAL: . . . [N]othing shall be wanting on the part of the Government to aid you in your efforts to regain possession of the territory from which we have been driven. . . . [T]he imperative demand for prompt and vigorous action arises . . . from the necessity of reoccupying the country. . . .

Of the immediate measures to be adopted in attaining this end . . . you must be the best judge. . . .

I remain, very respectfully and truly yours,

JEFFN. DAVIS.[12]

Johnston's intentions are manifested in a quote from his letter of 13 March 1864, to Lieutenant General Longstreet (then commanding Confederate forces in East Tennessee northeast of Knoxville):

In writing to the President on this subject, I expressed the opinion that the only practicable mode of assuming the offensive here seemed to me to be to wait for the enemy's advance, and if we beat him, follow into Middle Tennessee, it being much easier to beat him in Georgia than beyond the Cumberland Mountains and the results of victory much greater.[13]

On March 19, 1864, he wrote General Bragg, President Davis's chief of staff:

I believe fully, however, that Grant will be ready to act before we can be. . . . I would have the troops assembled here without delay, to repulse Grant's attack and then make our own, or should the enemy not take the initiative, do it ourselves. . . .

Should not the movement from Mississippi precede any advance from this point, so much as to enable those troops to cross the Tennessee before we move? Lieutenant-General Polk thought at the end of February that he could send 15,000 cavalry on such an expedition. Even two-thirds of that force might injure the railroads enough to compel the evacuation of Chattanooga; certainly it could make a powerful diversion.[14]

Foremost in Johnston's mind was a defense in place, to be followed by a counterattack after defeating the Union advance. He would hope for a Union direct attack that he could defeat with heavy casualties and a cavalry raid by Forrest to destroy Union supply lines. This hope would be the constant theme in Johnston's mind during the succeeding months.

END-OF-CHAPTER NOTES

1. Craig L. Symonds, *Joseph E. Johnston: A Civil War Biography* (New York: W. W. Norton and Company, 1992), 90.
2. General Robert E. Lee to President Davis, as quoted in William R. Scaife, *The Campaign for Atlanta* (Atlanta, Georgia: Civil War Publications, 1985), 45.
3. Brian Steel Wills, *A Battle from the Start* (New York: HarperCollins, 1992), 196.
4. 32 *OR* 3:837.
5. 32 *OR* 3:767.
6. Diary of Captain Thomas J. Key, as quoted in Castel, 106.
7. 32 *OR* 3:789.
8. 32 *OR* 3:839.
9. 32 *OR* 3:685–6.
10. 32 *OR* 3:840.
11. 31 *OR* 3:842.
12. 31 *OR* 3:856.
13. 32 *OR* 3:619.
14. 32 *OR* 3:654–5.

CHAPTER 13

What Actually Happened

RECAPITULATION OF SHERMAN'S PLAN

As stated earlier, Sherman actually chose course of action A7, a turning movement through Snake Creek Gap. He sent McPherson (with approximately 26,000 soldiers and 60 cannon but no cavalry because Garrard's division had not yet joined them) through the gap while holding Johnston's attention with the rest of his army group. Thomas (with 67,000 infantrymen, 102 cannon) attacked and took Tunnel Hill, then conducted supporting attacks against Buzzard's Roost, the northern end of Rocky Face, and Dug Gap. Schofield (with approximately 12,000 infantry, some cavalry, and 24 cannon) conducted a supporting attack against Dalton from the north in Crow Creek Valley. McPherson's orders were to move "to Snake Creek Gap, secure it and from it make a bold attack on the enemy's flank and his railroad at any point between Tilton and Resaca."[1] Sherman hoped to trap Johnston's army, forcing it either to retreat east into the mountains or to attack against great odds, causing the army's destruction either way.

ACTUAL OUTCOME OF THE PLAN

Sherman's plan worked perfectly at first, then ran into problems. Thomas took Tunnel Hill, securing the vital tunnel itself, and made strong demonstrations against Buzzard's Roost, Rocky Face, and Dug Gap. The supporting attack up the spine of Rocky Face from the north gained some ground before being stopped cold by Confederate soldiers. The attack by Geary's Division, Hooker's XXth Corps, against a small force at Dug Gap caused Johnston to move a reserve division under General Cleburne to its relief. Schofield, his right flank connected to Thomas' left, attacked from the north down Crow Creek Valley but attained no real success.

However, Johnston's attention was fully engaged by these supporting attacks. McPherson came up and took Snake Creek Gap without a fight (except for a small cavalry skirmish at the gap's exit). Then, attacking Resaca within a half-mile of the railroad, he hit strong resistance from a reinforced Confederate brigade under Brigadier General Cantey. Cantey's brigade had just moved to Resaca from Rome where it had been a few days earlier. McPherson, whose orders gave him latitude to withdraw back to Snake Creek Gap if he felt threatened, hesitated and then retreated. Lacking cavalry to give him early warning of any possible attack by the bulk of Johnston's army coming down behind him from the north and meeting stronger than expected resistance at Resaca, he decided to move back to Snake Creek Gap, where he could build strong defensive positions and protect his flanks using the rugged terrain.

This entire episode raises two controversial questions:

1. **Why did Johnston fail to post troops at Snake Creek Gap?** Contemporary accounts—and a personal reconnaissance—convince me that a relatively small force could have held the gap for a long time. Johnston and his adjutant general both had excuses for not guarding the gap and the message traffic ambiguously supports their contention that Wheeler was told to outpost the area but did not. The same messages can be read to infer that Dug Gap was the area of concern, not Snake Creek Gap. (See, for instance, 38 *OR* 4:664, 672, 673, and 681.) Some have suggested that Johnston did not know the gap was practical for the movement of large forces. Snake Creek Gap did not appear on some wartime maps until they were updated after the campaign.[2] Either way, Johnston is responsible: either he failed to perform proper reconnaissance on his area when he had the time earlier in the year (and therefore did not know about the gap), or his orders to Wheeler were too vague and not properly followed up.

2. **Why did McPherson retreat from Resaca when he outnumbered the defenders by a factor of at least five-to-one?** McPherson could have cut Johnston's supply lines easily, trapping the Confederate army and possibly sealing its fate. However, he had no cavalry and only a small mounted infantry unit to reconnoiter to the north—the direction of the bulk of Johnston's army—because Garrard's cavalry was not yet up. McPherson was very concerned about the strong infantry resistance at Resaca and about the potential of the entire Confederate army attacking him from the north, cutting him off from the gap and Sherman. Such an attack could possibly destroy the Army of the Tennessee

before Sherman could rescue him. It was McPherson's first experience at the army level—he had been a corps commander—and he was cautious. Details of his side of the story are not known, because McPherson was killed two months later on 22 July, east of Atlanta. Sherman, although greatly disappointed by the outcome, agreed that McPherson had acted within his orders. McPherson, listening to the voice of caution, missed the opportunity of a lifetime.

After these controversial episodes, Sherman decided to reinforce McPherson with all but one corps of Thomas's army and with the infantry of Schofield's army. It took several days to move these troops through Snake Creek Gap, during which time Johnston received more reinforcements from Polk and held onto Dalton, facing Howard's corps and Stoneman's cavalry. Finally, on the night of 12–13 May, Johnston realized the situation and retreated to defensive positions around Resaca, barely avoiding being cut off when Sherman advanced the bulk of the force from Snake Creek Gap again toward Resaca.

Sherman then attacked the lines Johnston quickly established around Resaca—the Battle of Resaca, 14–15 May—and Johnston counterattacked, but neither side had more than local success. After the battle of Resaca both generals were faced with new decisions: how should they accomplish their respective missions in light of the results of the first part of the campaign?

THE BALANCE OF THE CAMPAIGN

Interestingly, both generals maintained their respective campaign plans: Johnston stayed on the defensive, hoping that Sherman would conduct a frontal attack and that Forrest would be ordered to attack Sherman's supply lines. Unfortunately for Johnston, Forrest was never unleashed against Union railroads, because Sherman had arranged for Union raids into Mississippi that pinned Forrest in place.

Sherman conducted supporting attacks on Johnston's principal positions while sending McPherson to turn Johnston's position from the west, all the way from Dalton to the Chattahoochee. Then, in accordance with his original plans made as early as 10 April, he reversed his basic maneuver. "Should Johnston fall behind the Chattahoochee I would feign to the right, but pass to the left, and act on Atlanta, or on its eastern communications, according to developed facts."[3] After reaching the Chattahoochee, that is exactly what he did, having McPherson cross at Roswell, north of Atlanta. As for his constant use of McPherson as the maneuver element, remember that Sherman had commanded the Army of the Tennessee (now under McPherson) until Grant was called east. He trusted them more than any of his other soldiers and gave them the most important jobs almost all the time.

Map 13.1 illustrates the balance of the campaign, as explained in table 13.1. McPherson's movements are shown as solid arrows, Thomas's and Schofield's as dashed arrows.

TABLE 13.1 *The Campaign*

Stage/ Confederate Position	Maneuver	Supporting Attack	Outcome
1. Dalton 7–12 May	McPherson turned position via Snake Creek Gap	Thomas and Schofield threatened frontal attack	Johnston retreated to position 2 due to threat to his rear
2. Resaca 13–15 May	McPherson attacked first, then crossed Oostanaula River on Confederate left	Thomas and Schofield attacked, then threatened further attack	Johnston retreated to Adairsville, then Cassville, due to McPherson's threat to his rear
3. Cassville 16–20 May	No maneuver; Sherman pursued on two axes and almost was ambushed by Johnston north of Cassville but Hood failed to attack as ordered		After attack failure, Johnston wanted to defend but Hood and Polk convinced him to retreat to Allatoona
4. Allatoona 21–23 May	McPherson turned the Etowah position by crossing the river to the west and moving to Dallas	Demonstrated near Cartersville, then followed McPherson	Johnston moved to position 5, stopping turning movement

continued

TABLE 13.1 *The Campaign, continued*

Stage/ Confederate Position	Maneuver	Supporting Attack	Outcome
5. Dallas, New Hope Church, Pickett's Mill 24 May– 7 June	Frontal attacks failed, so McPherson turned Johnston's position to the east, moving back to railroad at Big Shanty	Frontal attacks failed	Johnston defeated attacks, but moved back to Kennesaw (position 6) when turning movement threatened the railroad
6. Pine and Lost Mountains, Kennesaw 11 June– 1 July	Frontal attacks won minor success, then failed, so maneuver (not McPherson this time) enveloped Confederate left	Frontal attacks failed	Johnston defeated initial attack, but was unable to extend his line on the left to stop the envelopment and retreated
7. Howell's Ferry 3–9 July	McPherson turned river position via Roswell	Demonstration held Confederates in position	Johnston retreated to Peachtree Creek, just north of Atlanta
8. Peachtree Creek 10–18 July	McPherson approached Atlanta via Decatur to the east	Held against Confederate attacks	Johnston relieved of command, Hood launched strong but unsuccessful attacks

MAP 13.1 *The Actual Campaign, Numbers Keyed to Text*

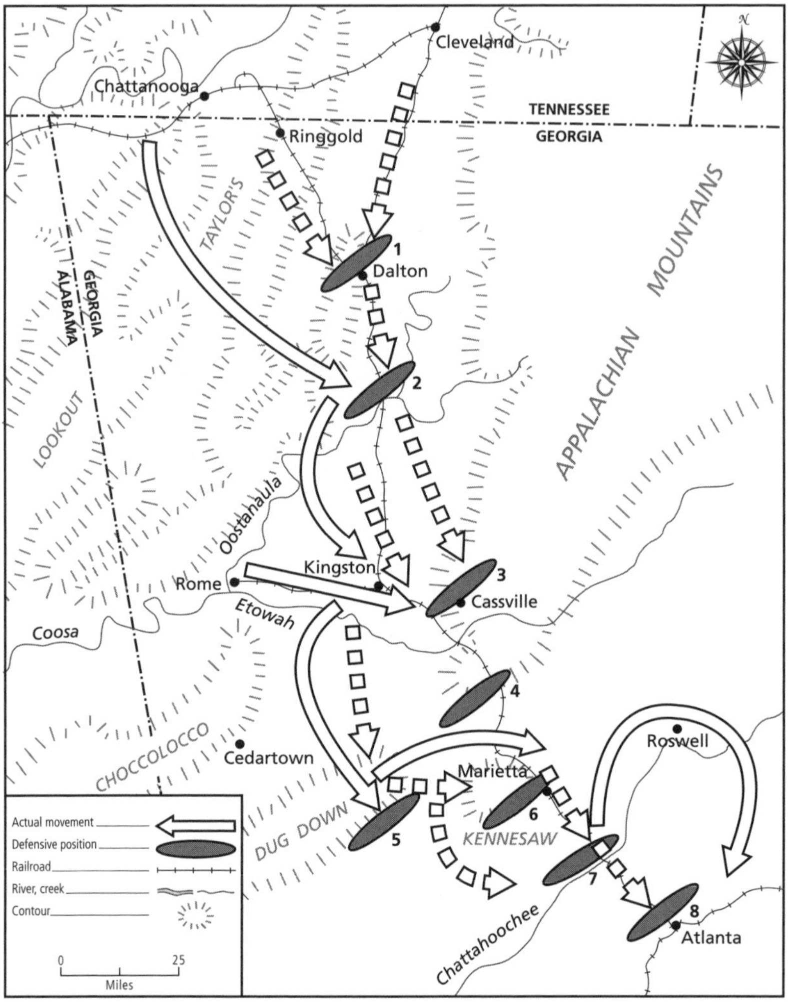

END-OF-CHAPTER NOTES

1. 38 *OR* 4:39.
2. Cox, 31.
3. 32 *OR* 3:313–4.

CHAPTER 14

Conclusions

ISSUES

Did General Sherman articulate a viable campaign plan?

B y now, the reader will have his or her own opinion. As originally explained in chapter 3 and summarized here. A campaign plan describes "a series of major operations arranged in time, space, and purpose to achieve a strategic objective."[1] It is the primary means that the overall commander uses to achieve unity of effort. The commander uses it to:

- define objectives and possible end states
- describe concepts of operation and sustainment
- arrange operations and assign tasks
- organize forces and establish command relationships

Sherman clearly had a campaign plan in mind; he just as clearly committed only the first phase of it to paper (see chapter 11). For this first phase, he organized his forces and established command relationships. He arranged the operations and assigned specific tasks to his subordinate armies. He described the overall concept of the operation and—in letters not included in this book—the concept of sustainment. Although he defined objectives for each subordinate army, he did not lay out possible end states other than those addressed in his contingency plans (Confederate attack on one wing of the army or Confederate retreat). He did not do so because the idea of the commander defining possible end states, including the desired end state, is relatively new in American military thought. Despite this omission, General Sherman's campaign plan was viable at least through the first phase of operations. As Joint Publication 3-0, *Doctrine for Joint Operations*, states: "Campaign planning . . . is based on *evolving* assumptions"[2] [italics added]. It would have been difficult for Sherman to plan much beyond where he did because too many uncertainties were in the way.

Did Sherman's campaign plan arrange its operations to achieve a strategic objective?

Grant defined Sherman's strategic objectives:

- Break up Johnston's army
- Get into the interior and damage war resources

Here it is possible to have different opinions. For instance, Albert Castel, in his definitive book *Decision in the West: The Atlanta Campaign of 1864*, thought Sherman ignored Grant's guidance to break up Johnston's army in favor of turning Johnston out of successive positions. That is certainly what happened. Castel felt that Grant had directed an attrition strategy based on breaking up Johnston's army first, then moving into the interior of Georgia to damage war resources. In the event, Johnston's army was not destroyed until Hood (who replaced Johnston by President Davis's orders when the armies were close to Atlanta) sent his soldiers on a series of bloody and doomed attacks, first against Sherman in the vicinity of Atlanta, then (after losing Atlanta) against Franklin, Tennessee, and Nashville.

In the author's opinion, had McPherson boldly executed his part of Sherman's plan, a rarity in the Civil War—a truly decisive battle— would have been fought. The attrition on the battlefield would have taken place on terms favorable to Sherman—something that would not necessarily have been true if Sherman had decided on a frontal attack or penetration. Sherman would have broken Johnston, sending the remnants of his army into the Appalachians and opening the way to Atlanta and the interior of Georgia. McPherson's timidity, coupled with Johnston's ability in extracting his army once he realized his situation, kept Johnston's army intact and Sherman out of the agricultural and industrial heart of Georgia until the fall of 1864.

EPILOGUE

General Sherman has been called "the first modern general."[3] Even though he did not have access to a modern staff or its procedures, he showed great ability to make decisions and supervise his army in a manner easily recognizable to modern military analysts. His plans did not always work out in exact detail—few plans do—but his sound planning and innate flexibility enabled him to turn Johnston out of strong positions. He accomplished his mission.

Hopefully you have gained an appreciation for modern military planning—and an even greater appreciation for those who had to plan without the benefit of modern staffs and their methods. If you have enjoyed this book, much of its purpose will have been accomplished.

END-OF-CHAPTER NOTES

1. von Clausewitz, 119–120.
2. Joint Pub 3-0, *Doctrine for Joint Operations* (Washington, D.C.: The Joint Staff, 1995), III-5.
3. Personal conversation with Professor Jay Luvaas, U.S. Army War College, 1993.

APPENDIX A

Organization of a Staff Ride

As stated in the preface, military units often conduct "staff rides," the purpose of which is to train the unit staff by using a real military battle or campaign as a vehicle for study. This appendix contains hints on how to conduct a staff ride based on the first stage of the Atlanta Campaign. The hints derive from having conducted a staff ride for the 20th Special Forces Group (Airborne) in 1995 using a preliminary draft of this book. Included are suggestions for a read-ahead package, the conduct of the classroom portion of the training, and a tour. The classroom portion of the staff ride will occupy much of the time allotted because of the emphasis on campaign planning.

READ-AHEAD

At least one week prior to the actual conduct of the staff ride, the principal trainer should issue each participant a read-ahead package. The purpose of this package is to familiarize the participant with the overall situation prior to his or her starting the staff ride.

The recommended read-ahead package consists of chapters 1, 2, 3, 4, and 6. Also, a copy of the table in the preface ("Estimate of the Situation"), maps 5.2–6.3, and (optionally) the photographs should be given to each participant. A useful preliminary debate could be scheduled using chapter 3 as a basis—soldiers will have fruitful discussions about some of the issues raised there.

If the principal trainer intends for each participant to play a specific role (such as logistics officer or intelligence officer), each participant could use the read-ahead information to form a staff estimate in that specific area for use during the classroom phase. This staff estimate would, of course, be a situational estimate prepared prior to the staff receiving the mission.

CLASSROOM

The classroom portion will be the core of the staff ride. Considerations in planning the classroom portion include scheduling a terrain orientation, locating an appropriate classroom, and setting up requirements and their schedule. The classroom training can be done before or without visiting the campaign area, but a better result (and fewer distractions) can be obtained by moving the staff ride group to the area. A preliminary terrain orientation prior to any classroom work would help set the stage. On the other hand, if done at the home station, participants may be able to use computers in lieu of butcher paper and perhaps come up with a better product more quickly. The classroom portion will take one training day.

TERRAIN ORIENTATION

On 30 April 1864, General Sherman rode to the top of Lookout Mountain and surveyed the landscape. Although by this time he had already made his plans and taken certain preliminary actions, this date is a convenient marker for the start of the campaign. Those who can tour the campaign area and wish to visit General Sherman's vantage point can reach it by taking Tennessee Highway 58 (Alton Park Boulevard) south from downtown Chattanooga and following the "Rock City" signs. The highway turns into Georgia 157 near the top of the mountain. Sherman's actual vantage point probably was the seven-state overlook within Rock City, a commercial establishment that charges admission, but a view almost as good can be obtained from two parking spots on the side of the highway just below the mountain crest. Rock City's phone number is (706) 820-2531.

In winter, a view from Sherman's most advanced positions can be obtained from the property of the Georgia State Forestry fire tower located on White Oak Mountain—the extension of Taylor's Ridge north of Ringgold Gap, just east of Ringgold. Take U.S. Highway 41 East. About one mile east of the Ringgold railroad station, Clearview Drive branches to the north (left). At the top of the ridge (about 1 mile), turn left to the fire tower. Advance coordination with the forester and the Sheriff's department in Ringgold is advised. When leaves are on the trees, there is no good vantage point except from the tower itself or from private homes.

MAP A.1 *Map, Ringgold to Rocky Face.*

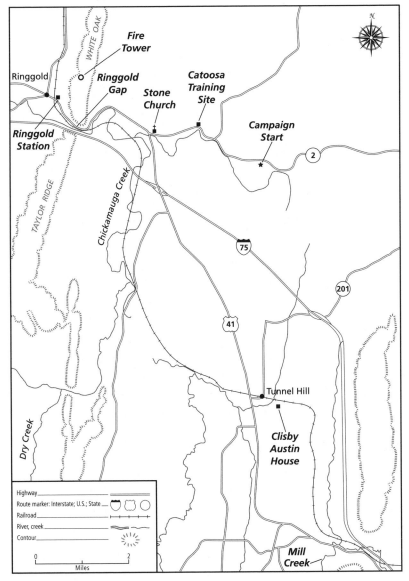

POSSIBLE TRAINING LOCATIONS

To conduct the classroom portion of the staff ride, a room with sufficient space is needed. There must be a place for a viewgraph projector, wall space to post sheets of butcher paper, and tables with chairs sufficient to accommodate the number of participants. Administrative areas such as a break area, a rest room, and a place to eat lunch are recommended.

The park building at Point Park in Chattanooga is a possible location from which to discuss Sherman's estimate of the situation. There is a small classroom there. Other locations include the Chickamauga National Military Park and the Catoosa National Guard Training Site. The Chickamauga Park is very interesting itself, and offers many exhibits of all kinds as well as some classroom space. Point Park is run by the National Park Service out of the Chickamauga National Battlefield. The Point Park phone number is (423) 821-7786, and the Chickamauga number is (706) 866-9241. The Chickamauga Park ranger must authorize any use of Point Park.

Military groups wishing to visit the area and stay overnight may also want to use the Catoosa Training Site, a Tennessee National Guard training site which has open-bay barracks for 240 men, 20 Bachelor Enlisted Quarters (BEQ) rooms, 35 Bachelor Officer Quarters (BOQ) rooms, two mess halls, and one classroom building. The telephone number is (706) 935-4897. The Catoosa facility, located east of Ringgold, is available most Mondays through Thursdays but may not be available on weekends due to prior training commitments.

ORGANIZATION

The participants should be divided into workgroups of no fewer than three people. At least three workgroups are recommended, but more than six probably would be impractical. For larger groups, multiple classrooms and instructors are needed.

First Requirement

After the participants are organized, each workgroup should be issued the first requirement, "Determining the Mission." If possible, each participant is given a personal copy of pp. 65–73 and map 5.1. At a minimum, each workgroup should have a copy of the pages, their read-ahead package, and either a transparency or a butcher paper chart on which to write their solution.

Workgroups are given 25 minutes to read the material (they can skip the example and go straight to Sherman's Mission), agree on Sherman's specified and implied tasks, and formulate a restated mission. Then each workgroup will, in turn, take two minutes to present their solution to the entire assemblage. The groups must then collectively agree, under the leadership of the principal trainer and by majority vote if necessary, on a restated mission.

With this mission in mind, each workgroup will discuss the preliminary staff estimates prepared earlier if that was done. The completion of the entire requirement (including discussion) will take 45 minutes to an hour.

Second Requirement

The second requirement is "Enumerating Enemy Capabilities." Each participant should be issued pp. 101–3, tables 7.3 and 7.5, and maps 7.1 and 7.3. The same procedure as that of the first requirement is followed, although a 35-minute period is allowed for the groups to formulate capabilities before presenting.

This is an appropriate time for determining those specific capabilities to be used later during the analysis phase. After the list of capabilities has been agreed upon, issue pp. 117–19 and allot 10 minutes for each group to choose capabilities for further analysis and 15 minutes for general discussion. The final list of capabilities to consider should number no more than two or three; otherwise, the wargaming phase will become unwieldy.

After the assemblage has agreed upon enemy capabilities, copies of Sherman's letters (pp. 108 and 109) should be issued to each group so that they can see what Sherman's opinion was. This requirement will take one and a half hours.

Third Requirement

"Determining Sherman's Courses of Action" is the third requirement. Each participant needs pp. 112–13 (with a warning to use their own restated mission, not that in the text) and map 8.1. Follow the same procedure as that used for the first requirement except allow an hour for completion.

Fourth Requirement

"Analysis of Courses of Action" is the fourth requirement. Each participant will need to read pp. 117–18, 120, and 122–25. Each workgroup may be assigned some courses of action from requirement 3 to wargame against the enemy capabilities from requirement 2, or each workgroup may choose the courses of action that they would like to use in wargaming. The workgroup will use a transparency or butcher paper to describe the course of action in detail and illustrate their branches and sequels diagram. They will then list advantages and disadvantages, as determined by the war game, against the enemy capabilities chosen. An hour should be allotted for wargaming and a half hour for presenting results to all participants.

Fifth Requirement

To complete the "Comparison of Courses of Action and Decision" requirement, issue pp. 126–27, 131–35, and 138–41 to the workgroups. Each workgroup should choose significant factors first (with a note as to the rationale for choosing these factors), then, based on wargaming results, list in tabular form whether the factor is favorable to the courses of action of interest. The best course of action (in the workgroup's opinion) should be evident from this table. The workgroup should then sketch out the decision and concept of the operation (task organization, employment of units, command and control, contingencies, and liaison) on butcher paper and present this solution to the class. The fifth requirement should take about an hour and a half.

Wrap-up

After each workgroup presents an opinion, the instructor will need to present Sherman's solution (pp. 147–48) to the participants and, if desired, give them copies of the pages. Chapters 12 and 13 can also be issued to participants (giving the view from the other side and what happened) if the instructor desires. Additionally, if there is time available, the instructor may choose to introduce the key questions from chapter 14 and engender further discussion on campaign plans and critique of Sherman's plan. Some discussion of what actually happened during the opening phases of the campaign should take place prior to the battlefield tour.

Breaks should be taken individually during work sessions.

Timetable

Time	Activity	Reference pages
0730–0800	Introduction and Organization	Chapters 4, 6; preface table; and maps 5.2–6.3 should have been issued several days prior
0800–0900	1st requirement	Pages 65–73, map 5.1
0900–1030	2nd requirement	Pages 101–3, 108–9, 117–19, tables 7.3 and 7.5, maps 7.1 and 7.3
1030–1130	3rd requirement	Pages 112–13, map 8.1
1130–1230	Lunch	—
1230–1400	4th requirement	Pages 117–18, 120, 122–25
1400–1530	5th requirement	Pages 126-27, 131–35, 138–41
1530–1600	Wrap-up	Pages 145-48, chapters 12 and 13

TOUR

The tour of the initial portion of the campaign (up to the battle of Resaca) will take several hours, depending on the number of questions asked at each stop. If you intend to actually ride around on the battlefield instead of conducting a purely classroom exercise, a personal reconnaissance by the instructor(s) is essential. It would be helpful in any event.

Valuable references for the tour include Miles' *Fields of Glory: A History and Tour Guide of the Atlanta Campaign* and Scaife's *The Campaign for Atlanta*. Be careful with the directions, as sometimes east and west are transposed. The tour comprises two sections: the supporting attack (three prongs) and the turning movement. Start in Ringgold. To get to the start point, follow these directions:

From the intersection of Interstates 24 and 75 in Chattanooga, take I-75 south 6.5 miles to Georgia 2. Exit and turn left on Georgia 2 (Battlefield Parkway), going 1.4 miles to US 41. Turn right on US 41/GA 2 and drive 1.6 miles to the railroad station on the left. This station, damaged heavily during the war, is the start of the tour.

Supporting Attack

The supporting attack, a frontal attack, actually took place all along the line from Potato Hill on the far left to Dug Gap on the right. The tour will cover three axes of advance: the Army of the Ohio (Schofield's) attack down Crow Creek Valley, the XIV Corps (Palmer's) attack against Tunnel Hill, and the XX Corps (Hooker's) attack against Dug Gap. The IV Corps (Howard's) attack along the spine of Rocky Face Ridge is not followed, as there is no easy path there.

SCHOFIELD'S ATTACK

The first segment, covering Schofield's attack, starts at the Ringgold Railroad Station (map A.1). Exit the station parking lot, set the odometer to zero, and turn left on GA 2/US 41 South. After 0.5 miles on the right is a small parking area with picnic tables and a monument. This is the Ringgold Gap Historical Site with plaques commemorating the campaign. This gap is the location of the front lines of the Army of the Cumberland (Baird's 3rd Division, Palmer's XIV Corps) at the start of the campaign.

Reset the odometer and turn right on GA 2/US 41. Go 1.9 miles to where GA 2 splits to the left and turn left into the drive of the Old Stone Presbyterian Church. This church was here during the campaign and had actually been used as a hospital after Chickamauga. Now continue east on GA 2, passing Catoosa National Guard Training Site on your left 0.9 miles beyond the church. On the right 3.6 miles beyond the Stone Church is a historical marker commemorating the start of the Atlanta Campaign. North of the road on the high ground was Dr. Lee's house, where Sherman, Thomas, and Schofield met and watched Howard's IV Corps move forward to attack Rocky Face Ridge.

Reset the odometer and continue east on GA 2. After 3.1 miles is a stop sign and store at Varnell's Station on the Eastern Tennessee and Georgia (now Southern) Railroad. Pick up map A.2. Schofield's Army of the Ohio advanced along and west of the railroad through Varnell.

From the stop sign, reset the odometer and turn south following GA 2; at 0.1 miles south of Varnell, GA 2 turns east and GA 201 continues south. Follow GA 201 parallel to the railroad. On GA 201 2.2 miles south of Varnell, Reed Road branches to the left. Take Reed Road south. After 0.8 miles note a historical marker on the left entitled "Military Operations in Crow Valley."

Map A.2 *Map, Crow Creek Valley*

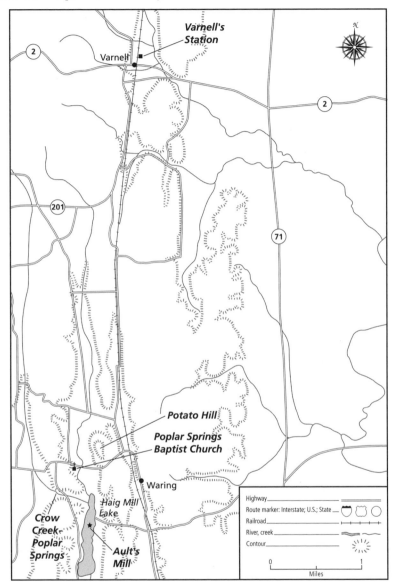

MAP A.3 *Map, Mill Creek Valley*

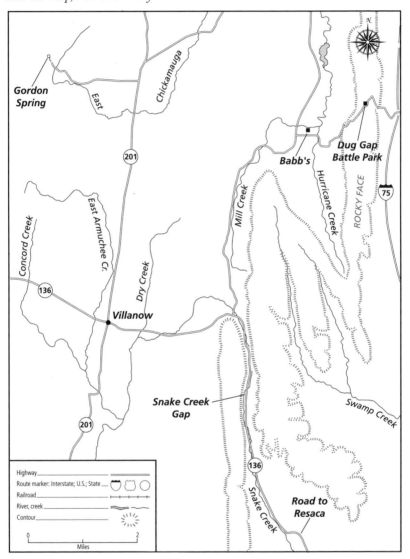

Rounding the next curve, you will notice a prominent hill in the distance in front of you. This is Potato Hill, the anchor of the Confederate right and the site (on the northwestern slope) of Rowan's Georgia Light Battery—four 12-pound Napoleon smoothbores—during the fight.

In this area (a mile north of Potato Hill) on 8 May, Martin's Division of Wheeler's Cavalry Corps attacked McCook's Cavalry Division, which was screening in front of Schofield. McCook was routed, the 1st Wisconsin Cavalry Regiment lost 151 men, and the entire division had to fall back on the infantry.

At a distance of 3.1 miles from the Georgia 201, Reed intersects Poplar Springs Road. Turn right on it and go another 0.35 miles into the parking lot of the Poplar Springs Baptist Church on the left. This high ground was the site of the defensive lines of Mercer's Georgia Brigade, Walker's Division of Hardee's Corps. Schofield made five demonstration attacks against this line on 9 May, but none of them as pressed seriously and they made no dent in the Confederate lines.

Continue west on Poplar Springs Road 0.5 miles until it intersects with Crow Creek Valley Road. At the intersection, face south looking down Crow Creek Valley Road. The Confederate line curved around the hill to your left to the south, then extended across the valley about 400 meters (a quarter of a mile) south of you to the crest of Rocky Face ridge to your right front. While Schofield's Army of the Ohio was attacking in the valley, Harker's Brigade of the 2nd (Newton's) Division of the IV Corps was unsuccessfully assaulting Pettus's Alabama Brigade of Stevenson's Division, Hood's Corps, attacking south along the knife edge of the ridge. Ault's Mill, Hardee's headquarters during the supporting attack, has been covered by the lake shown on the map.

This intersection is the end of the tour of Schofield's portion of the supporting attack. To return to take up Palmer's attack, continue west on Poplar Springs Road. The road turns north, paralleling the ridge. After another 2.6 miles, intersect New Hope Road and turn left, crossing the low extension of Rocky Face Ridge. Going west on New Hope Road for 1.2 miles to GA 201, you are essentially reversing the route that Harker's Brigade took during their attack. Turn left on GA 201 to Interstate 75 and turn right (north) on it. Exit at Exit 345 (US 41). This is where the tour of the XIV (Palmer's) Corps attack starts.

PALMER'S ATTACK

Reset the odometer at the intersection of Interstate 75 and US 41. Drive south on US 41 towards Tunnel Hill, the location of part of Wheeler's cavalry prior to the start of the campaign. Map A.1 shows the area. Wheeler made no effort to defend Tunnel Hill from Palmer, merely demonstrating with horse artillery (probably a two-gun section of Ferrell's Battery) and a few skirmishers.

US 41 crosses over the rail line 3.9 miles from the start. Turn left immediately on Oak Street and go straight. Oak Street turns to the left, but you need to go straight ahead on Clisby Austin Road. At that intersection to your left, next to a parking lot, there are three historical markers concerned with the campaign. After crossing a modern covered bridge, there will be a paved parking lot on the left, 0.5 miles from US 41. Park there. To your south about 250 meters is the Clisby Austin house, where Sherman established his headquarters after Palmer seized Tunnel Hill. Follow the asphalt path east, parallel to the railroad. The path leads to the old tunnel (the new railroad tunnel is adjacent to the old one and on its left), but the pathway may be blocked by a locked barrier.

Although the Confederate Army did take up the tracks, no attempt was made to damage the tunnel itself. The tunnel was invaluable to Sherman's efforts to supply his army later in the campaign. Johnston probably did not give orders to destroy the tunnel because—had he beaten Sherman and counterattacked north—he would have needed it as well. Destroying the tunnel would have told his army and Jefferson Davis both that he did not expect to defeat Sherman.

Return to US 41, resetting the odometer there. Turn left on US 41 (be very careful, because the southbound traffic is difficult to see). After 3.5 miles, you will cross Mill Creek, which the Confederate Army had dammed to form a pond as a barrier across the front of the pass. There is a historical marker on the left (north) side of the road. At 4.1 miles (slow down or you'll miss it!), turn right into the Georgia State Patrol post. In front of the building is another memorial to the campaign. This ground was held by Stewart's Division of Hood's Corps, Baker's Alabama Brigade on the high ground to the north, and Gibson's Louisiana Brigade on the south side of the pass. Oliver's Eufaula Alabama Battery (four 3-inch rifles) occupied Redoubt Fisk blocking the road. The Union 1st (Johnson) and 2nd (Davis) Divisions of the XIV Corps demonstrated against these positions on 8 May, attacking from the west and supported by two batteries on Blue Mountain 2 kilometers (over 1 mile) to the west of the gap. Johnston hoped that Sherman would seriously attack here (he was envious of Lee's victory in similar circumstances at Fredericksburg, Virginia, a year and a half earlier), but this again was merely an attempt by Sherman to fix Johnston in position.

This is the end of the tour of the XIV Corps (Palmer's) attack. It is necessary to go back across Mill Creek to reach the next start point. Turn right out of the Georgia State Patrol parking lot, go into Dalton (for a quick break and a safe turn-around), then turn back and head west on US 41. Reset the odometer as you pass the Georgia State Patrol entrance. Go 1.1 miles, then turn left on Old Lafayette Road just past the light. Go another 0.6 miles to Mill Creek Road and take a left. After 5 miles, there will be a historical marker on the left for Babb's plantation, which was there during the campaign, and a battle marker. Drive another 0.2 miles south on Mill Creek Road until you reach Hurricane Road and pull into the Mill Creek Baptist Church parking lot to your left front.

HOOKER'S ATTACK

Geary's 2nd Division (about 7,000 men present for duty) of Hooker's XX Corps crossed Taylor's Ridge through a gap about 11 kilometers (7 miles) west of your current position near Gordon Spring. Map A.3 shows the terrain. No road crosses Taylor's Ridge there now, but there was a road in 1864. Geary advanced to just north of your current location (Babb's) on 8 May, sent one brigade southwest to cover McPherson's advance, and retained two brigades with him.

Drive east on Hurricane Road 0.8 miles, then turn left up Dug Gap Road and continue for 1.5 miles. Geary attacked up this road with two brigades—almost 5,000 men. Waiting at the top were the 1st and 2nd Arkansas Mounted Infantry Regiments and Grigsby's Cavalry Brigade, a total of fewer than 1,000 men after horse-holders were taken out of the line.

Turn left into the Dug Gap Battle Park (operated by the Whitfield-Maury Historical Society and the Civil War Round Table of Dalton). Coordinate ahead of time to get the gate opened. The steep rock palisades to the south and the stone wall (built by Grigsby's men) to the north outline the Confederate positions. Geary, supported by McGill's Pennsylvania Light Battery E (four 3-inch rifles) near Babb's, attacked

MAP A.4 *Map, Resaca, USGS*

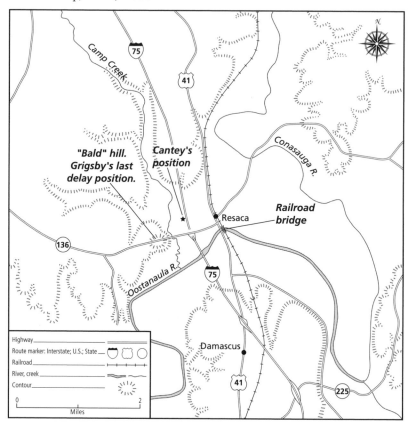

three times but the terrain and fierce resistance stymied the attack. Geary lost 357 men, the Confederates "not a score." The Confederates almost ran out of ammunition, but made up for it by rolling large rocks down on Geary's men. The arrival of Confederate reinforcements, two brigades of Cleburne's Division, Hardee's Corps, ended the attack and any threat to the position, just before dark on the eighth.

This ends the tour of the supporting attack areas. Return down the mountain to the intersection of Hurricane Road and Mill Creek Road. Reset the odometer and turn left (south) on Mill Creek Road. Go 1.8 miles and turn left on Lower Mill Creek Road. (Be careful here. The map shows the main road going to the left, but actually the main road goes straight and it is easy to miss the turn-off.) Continue on Lower Mill Creek Road 3.45 miles to GA 136, being careful not to angle right on Villanow Mill Creek Road when it branches off to the right. Three miles

(5 kilometers) to the west of Lower Mill Creek Road on GA 136 is the village of Villanow. McPherson's Army of the Tennessee, conducting their turning movement, marched through Villanow, along present-day GA 136 to your current position just short of Snake Creek Gap.

Turning Movement

Turn left on GA 136 and drive 5 miles through Snake Creek Gap to the GA 136-GA 136 Connection intersection at the gap's southern end. There is a historical marker on the left (east) side of the road there.

On 8 May, Sweeny's 2nd Division of Dodge's XVI Corps marched for more than 20 miles through Villanow and through Snake Creek Gap, bivouacking at the south end of the gap. Three other divisions of McPherson's Army of the Tennessee reached the north end of the gap. Sweeny was only 7 miles (11 kilometers) from Resaca and the railroad bridge over the Oostanaula River.

At dawn on 9 May, Grigsby's Cavalry Brigade, fresh from the Dug Gap fight, arrived to find Sweeny. A report had reached Johnston about McPherson's movement and he had dispatched the only cavalry he had on that flank to determine the situation and report it. Grigsby immediately started a delay, while sending a message back to Resaca. Cantey's Alabama Brigade of approximately 1,600 men and four Napoleon guns was at Resaca, soon to be joined by Reynolds' Arkansas Brigade (of Polk's Army of Mississippi), about the same strength, and another battery of four Napoleon guns. Total Confederate strength in and around Resaca was fewer than 5,000, facing McPherson's 25,000.

Go east on GA 136 for 6 miles. The hills on the left and right of the road were the last delay positions held by Grigsby's men, reached by McPherson's men about 2 PM. In front of you and beyond Camp Creek, on ground now occupied by and east of Interstate 75, was Cantey's entrenched position. Just beyond are Resaca and the railroad bridge. By 4 PM, McPherson had two divisions (more than 12,000 men, plus artillery) up and started a move forward. A show of resistance made him change his mind and, worried about Johnston's army coming down from his north, he withdrew back to the mouth of Snake Creek Gap.

On 12 May Johnston withdrew his entire army to new lines around Resaca, and, reinforced by Polk, he and Sherman fought a pitched battle in the vicinity on 14 May.

CONCLUSION

Sherman's plan stood an excellent chance of destroying Johnston's army. However, he did not give his turning movement adequate strength (particularly in cavalry) and his subordinate McPherson, made cautious by this lack and by his relative inexperience, did not press his advantage. Modern commentators believe that if Thomas—who originally suggested Snake Creek Gap to Sherman—had made this attack with his entire Army of the Cumberland, it would have succeeded.

Military Symbols

The military symbols used in the book are basically the same as those in use by the U.S. Army today. The exception is that during the Civil War, many units (particularly Confederate units) were known by their commander's name, so in those cases the commander's name is written next to or beneath the unit, wherever there is room, instead of to the left of the symbol.

A friendly military unit is represented by a rectangle drawn so that its center is positioned approximately over the unit's actual location on the map. The rectangle is filled by a particular symbol that indicates the type of unit shown. If colors are used, both sides are represented by rectangles, friendly in blue and enemy in red. If colors are not available, enemy units are represented by a diamond or a double-line rectangle. For the Civil War, the following unit symbols are sufficient:

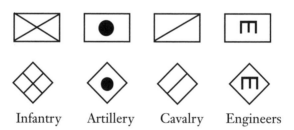

Infantry   Artillery   Cavalry   Engineers

The size of the unit is indicated by symbols on top of the rectangle.

XXXXX	Army Group
XXXX	Army
XXX	Corps
XX	Division
X	Brigade
I I I	Regiment
I I	Battalion
I	Company

For instance, this is the symbol for a friendly infantry division:

The identification of the unit is given by a number to the left of the rectangle or the commander's name below or next to the rectangle. Corps numbers are given in Arabic numerals on the map and usually by Roman numerals in text. For instance, the two following symbols were used in the text. Logan's Union XV Corps is on the left, and Martin's Confederate cavalry division is on the right.

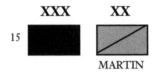

Glossary

The source is provided at the end of each definition. If the source is Gilham, the definition is circa 1861. Other sources are modern. If no source is cited, the definition is the author's.

adjutant general: Is the chief staff officer of the army, division, or brigade to which he belongs, and assists the general in the discharge of his duties; he keeps the roster of the officers; makes details for duty; makes up morning reports, returns, etc.; publishes the orders of the general; and is the channel through which all reports to, and correspondence with, the general pass. (Gilham, 1861)

administrative: Pertaining to the internal management of units. (Joint Staff, 1995 [Joint Pub 1-02])

agility: The ability to act and react faster than an opponent. (U.S. Dept. of the Army, 1993 [FM 100-5])

aide-de-camp: An officer appointed to attend a general officer; he receives and carries orders, and discharges such other duties as may be necessary. A Brigadier-General is entitled to one, and a Major-General to two aides-de-camp. (Gilham)

alliance: The result of formal agreements (i.e., treaties) between two or more nations for broad, long-term objectives that further the common interests of the members. (Joint Chiefs of Staff, 1995 [Joint Pub 5-0])

ammunition: implies everything in the way of powder, balls, shells, cartridges, canister and grape shot, etc. (Gilham)

army: An organized body of armed men commanded by a general. . . . An army is made up of a staff and administrative departments, and four distinct arms— Infantry, Cavalry, Artillery, and Engineers; each having distinct duties, but all combining to form one and the same military body. (Gilham)

army group: Several field armies under a designated commander. (Joint Pub 1-02)

artillery: Every sort of Fire-arms of large caliber, as guns, mortars, howitzers, etc., together with everything necessary for serving them in the field, at sieges, etc. Also a term applied to the science which treats of the construction and service of artillery. Also a name given to the troops which serve artillery. (Gilham)

assumption: A supposition on the current situation or a presupposition on the future course of events, either or both assumed to be true in the absence of positive proof, necessary to enable the commander in the process of planning to complete an estimate of the situation and make a decision on the course of action. (Joint Pub 1-02)

attack: An onset upon the enemy, either to gain a post, or break his ranks; or to divert his attention and make him divide his forces, when it becomes a *false attack*. (Gilham)

attrition: The reduction in the effectiveness of a force caused by loss of personnel and materiel. (Joint Pub 1-02)

audacity: Boldness or daring (Newell and Krause, 1994 [Random House])

base: A locality from which operations are projected or supported. (Joint Pub 1-02)

battalion: Any body of infantry from two companies to ten, and serving under the same commander. (Gilham)

battery: Tactical and administrative artillery unit corresponding to a company or similar unit in other branches of the Army. (Joint Pub 1-02)

battle: A series of related tactical engagements. (FM 100-5)

battlespace: A comprehensive, conceptual view of the operational environment and all factors that influence the success of a military operation. (FM 100-5)

blockade: The isolating of a place, especially a port, harbor, or part of a coast, by hostile ships or troops by preventing entrance or exit. (Newell and Krause)

bombardment: An attack or battering by artillery fire. (Random House)

branch: A contingency or option built into the basic plan. (FM 100-5)

brigade: A unit usually smaller than a division to which are attached groups and/or battalions [author's comment: in the Civil War, regiments] and smaller units tailored to meet anticipated requirements. (Joint Pub 1-02)

brigadier general: The commander of a brigade; an officer whose rank is next above that of a colonel. (Gilham)

caisson: A carriage for artillery ammunition; each piece of field artillery is followed by its caisson. (Gilham)

campaign: A series of related military operations aimed at accomplishing a strategic or operational objective within a given time and space (Joint Pub 1-02), or: The creative use of tactical activity—or the decision to forego tactical activity—to accomplish a particular strategic purpose, with a specific situational context, which most often includes an adaptive opponent. (FM 100-5)

cannon: A general term for every form of artillery. (Gilham)

capability: The ability to execute a specified course of action. (Joint Pub 1-02)

captain: The commander of a company. (Gilham)

cavalry: That portion of an army which serves and fights on horseback. (Gilham)

centers of gravity: Those characteristics, capabilities, or localities from which a military force derives its freedom of action, physical strength, or will to fight. (FM 100-5)

chaplain: An ecclesiastic attached to a military unit. (Random House)

colonel: The commander of a regiment. (Gilham)

combat: A battle. (Gilham)

combat efficiency: The state of preparedness to perform its combat mission of a military unit in terms of its morale, training, and equipment.

combined arms: The use of several combat arms (such as artillery and infantry) and supporting arms (such as engineers) in combination to achieve synergy and effects none could achieve alone.

command: The authority that a commander in the Military Service lawfully exercises over subordinates by virtue of rank or assignment. (Joint Pub 1-02)

commander's intent: A clear, concise statement of what the force must do to succeed with respect to the enemy and the terrain, and the desired end state. (FM 100-5)

commissary: An officer charged with the purchase and issue of provisions for the troops. (Gilham)

communications: The means of sending messages, orders, and so on. Also, routes and transportation for moving troops and supplies from a base to an area of operations.

company: A small body of from 50 to 100 men, and commanded by a captain. (Gilham)

concentration: The assembling of military forces in a particular area in preparation for further operations.

concept of the operation: The description of how a commander visualizes the major operation, battle, or engagement unfolding. (FM 100-5)

contingency: An emergency involving military forces caused by . . . required military operations. (Joint Pub 1-02)

control: Authority which may be less than full command exercised by a commander over part of the activities of subordinates or other organizations. (Joint Pub 1-02)

coordination: Harmonious combination or interaction.

corps: A body of troops acting together under one commander. (Gilham) In modern terms, a body of several divisions and other, supporting units.

counterattack: An attack made as an offset or reply to another attack.

courier: A messenger (usually a commissioned or warrant officer) responsible for the secure physical transmission and delivery of documents and material. (Joint Pub 1-02)

course of action: A plan that would accomplish, or is related to the accomplishment of, a mission. The scheme adopted to accomplish a task or mission. (Joint Pub 1-02)

cover: Shelter or protection, either natural or artificial. (Joint Pub 1-02)

culmination point: The point in time and space when the attacker's combat power no longer exceeds that of the defender or when the defender no longer has the capability to defend successfully. (FM 100-5)

deception: Those measures designed to mislead the enemy by manipulation, distortion, or falsification of evidence to induce him to react in a manner prejudicial to his interests. (Joint Pub 1-02)

decision: In an estimate of the situation, a clear and concise statement of the line of action intended to be followed by the commander as the one most favorable to the successful accomplishment of the mission. (Joint Pub 1-02)

decisive points: Physical elements or events in time that—when retained or controlled—offer a commander a marked advantage and greatly influence the outcome of an action. (FM 100-5)

defeat in detail: To destroy an enemy by concentrating the mass of your troops against separate detachments of his such that, although the armies may be nearly equal in strength or the enemy may outnumber you, during each separate engagement your troops significantly outnumber his.

defend: To ward off attack. (Random House)

defensive: Operations undertaken to cause an enemy attack to fail. Alone, they achieve no decision. They must ultimately be combined with or followed by offensive action. (FM 100-5)

delay: An operation in which a force under pressure trades space for time by slowing down the enemy's momentum and inflicting maximum damage on the enemy without, in principle, becoming decisively engaged. (Joint Pub 1-02)

demonstration: An attempt to deceive the enemy by letting him observe certain actions that would lead him to believe a particular activity is planned.

deploy: To display or spread out troops. (Gilham)

depot: An activity for the receipt, classification, storage, accounting, issue, maintenance, procurement, manufacture, assembly, research, salvage, or disposal of materiel. (Joint Pub 1-02)

depth: The extension of operations in time, space, resources, and purpose. (FM 100-5)

dispositions: Distribution of the elements of a command within an area, usually the exact location of each unit headquarters and the deployment of the forces subordinate to it. (Joint Pub 1-02)

diversion: The act of drawing the attention and forces of an enemy from the point of the principal operation; an attack, alarm, or feint that diverts attention. (Joint Pub 1-02)

division: A major administrative and tactical unit/formation which combines in itself the necessary arms and services required for sustained combat, larger than a regiment/brigade and smaller than a corps. (Joint Pub 1-02)

doctrine: Fundamental principles by which the military forces or elements thereof guide their actions in support of national objectives. It is authoritative but requires judgment in application. (Joint Pub 1-02)

economy-of-force: The employment of all combat power in the most effective way possible; allocation of minimum essential combat power to secondary efforts. (FM 100-5)

effective: Prepared and available for service. (Random House)

enciphered: Plain text converted into unintelligible form by means of a cipher system. (Joint Pub 1-02)

enclave: A country or especially an outlying portion of a country, entirely or mostly surrounded by the territory of another country. (Random House)

end state: The set of required conditions—diplomatic, informational, military, and economic—that achieve our national interests in a situation. (FM 100-5)

enfilade: To throw shot along the whole length of the enemy's line. (Gilham)

engagement: The application of military means to accomplish specific tasks. (FM 100-5)

engineer: Officers charged with planning, constructing, and repairing all fortifications and all defensive works; with planning the attack and defense of military works, etc. (Gilham)

entrench: To dig trenches for defensive purposes around. (Random House)

envelopment: An offensive maneuver in which the main attacking force passes around or over the enemy's principal defensive positions to secure objectives to the enemy's rear. (Joint Pub 1-02) Less deep than a turning movement.

estimate: An analysis of a foreign situation, development, or trend that identifies its major elements, interprets the significance, and appraises the future possibilities and the prospective results of the various actions that might be taken. (Joint Pub 1-02); significant facts and conclusions based on analyzed data. (FM 100-5)

exploitation: Taking advantage of and making permanent the temporary effects of battlefield success. (FM 100-5)

exterior lines: The necessity of moving reinforcements around enemy positions in order to support other friendly units. One is said to operate on exterior lines when one's reinforcements or reserve must take a long detour (such as around the outside of a circle) to reach another friendly position. Opposite of interior lines.

feint: A mock attack, made to conceal the true one. (Gilham)

firepower: The amount of fire which may be delivered by a position, unit, or weapon system. (Joint Pub 1-02)

flanks: The right and left of an army, encampment, battalion, company, etc. (Gilham)

flexibility: Ability to undergo modification or adaptation. (Adapted from Random House)

forage: The hay, straw, and oats required for the subsistence of the horses of an army. (Gilham)

force ratio: The number obtained by dividing the number of soldiers on one side by that of the other side.

frontal attack: An offensive maneuver in which the main action is directed against the front of the enemy forces. (Joint Pub 1-02)

general: All officers above the rank of colonel. The only grades in the U.S. service are brigadier-general, major-general, and lieutenant-general. (Gilham) The rank of general (4 stars) is now (2004) authorized and the rank of general of the army (5 stars) was used during World War II.

haversack: A linen bag worn to carry a soldier's provisions on the march. (Gilham)

indicator: An item of information which reflects the intention or capability of a potential enemy to adopt or reject a course of action. (Joint Pub 1-02)

infantry: Foot soldiers armed with the musket, or rifle. (Gilham)

infiltration: The movement through or into an area or territory occupied by . . . enemy troops . . . made, either by small groups or by individuals, at extended or irregular intervals . . . [C]ontact is avoided. (Joint Pub 1-02)

initiative: Setting or changing the terms of an operation by action; implies a bold, offensive spirit. (FM 100-5)

inspector general: An officer whose duty it is to inspect the troops at stated times, and report the state of their discipline, efficiency, etc. (Gilham)

intelligence: Information and knowledge about an adversary obtained through observation, investigation, analysis, or understanding. (Joint Pub 1-02)

interior lines: The ability to move reinforcements or reserves by a direct route to any friendly units (such as from one point to another on the interior of a circle).

interrogation: Systematic effort to procure information by direct questioning of a person under the control of the questioner. (Joint Pub 1-02)

invest: To seize upon all the avenues of approach to a place or town, so as to cut it off from succor. (Gilham)

judge advocate: A staff officer designated as legal advisor to a commander and charged with the administration of military justice. (Random House)

leadership: Ability to lead. (Random House)

liaison: That contact or intercommunication maintained between elements of military forces to ensure mutual understanding and unity of purpose and action. (Joint Pub 1-02)

lieutenant colonel: A commissioned officer ranking next below a colonel and next above a major. (Random House)

lieutenant general: An officer ranking next below a general and next above a major general. (Random House)

limber box: A two-wheeled vehicle, originally pulled by four or six horses, behind which is towed a field gun or caisson. (Random House)

line crosser: A soldier who deserts to the other army.

lines of communications: All the routes which connect an operating military force with a base of operations and along which supplies and military forces move. (Joint Pub 1-02)

lines of operations: The logical or geographical linkage of objectives or a series of objectives with the forces that must achieve them. (FM 100-5)

line of retreat: A clear path available to a military unit for it to use to move away from the enemy.

line of sight: An imaginary straight line running through the aligned sights of a firearm. (Random House)

logistics: The science of planning and carrying out the movement and maintenance of forces . . . [T]hose aspects of military operations which deal with . . . materiel, . . . personnel, . . . facilities, and . . . services. (Joint Pub 1-02); the movement and sustainment of operating forces. (FM 100-5)

major: An officer next in rank to a lieutenant colonel. (Gilham)

major general: An officer ranking next below a lieutenant general and next above a brigadier general. (Random House)

maneuver: Employment of forces on the battlefield through movement in combination with fire, or fire potential, to achieve a position of advantage in respect to the enemy in order to accomplish the mission. (Joint Pub 1-02)

maneuver warfare: The use of movement and deception to attack an enemy's vital points while avoiding his strength.

mass: The concentration of combat power in a decisive manner in time and space. (FM 100-5 and Joint Pub 1-02)

mines: Subterranean passages dug under the walls of a fortification, or under the works of a besieging army, for the purpose of blowing them up by means of gunpowder. (Gilham)

mission: The task, together with the purpose, that clearly indicates the action to be taken and the reason thereof. (Joint Pub 1-02)

morale: Fighting spirit. (FM 100-5)

musket: A heavy, large-caliber hand gun for infantry soldiers. (Random House)

objective: The physical object of the action taken; for example, a definite tactical feature, the seizure and/or holding of which is essential to the commander's plan (Joint Pub 1-02); a clearly defined, decisive, and attainable goal. (FM 100-5)

offensive: Operations that carry the fight to the enemy. They are the decisive form of warfare, the commander's ultimate means of imposing his will on the enemy. (FM 100-5)

Official Records (OR): *The War of the Rebellion: A Compilation of the Official Records of the Union and Confederate Armies*, in 128 volumes.

operational art: The employment of military forces to attain strategic and/or operational objectives through the design, organization, integration, and conduct of strategies, campaigns, major operations, and battles. Operational art translates the joint force commander's strategy into operational design, and, ultimately, tactical action, by integrating the key activities at all levels of war. (Joint Pub 1-02)

operational reach: The distance and duration in which we can successfully employ military capabilities. (FM 100-5)

operations: Military actions or the carrying out of strategic, tactical, service, training, or administrative military missions; the process of carrying on combat, including movement, supply, attack, defense, and maneuvers needed to gain the objectives of any battle or campaign. (Joint Pub 1-02)

orderly: An enlisted man selected to perform various menial chores for an officer or officers. (Random House)

orchestration: Arrange, develop, organize, or combine to achieve a desired or maximum effect. (FM 100-5)

ordnance: Explosives, chemicals, pyrotechnics, and similar stores; for example, bombs, guns and ammunition, flares, smoke, napalm. (Joint Pub 1-02)

outpost: Body of troops posted beyond the bounds or limits of the encampment. (Gilham)

parallels: The trenches or lines made by the besiegers around the works of the besieged. (Gilham)

penetration: A form of offensive which seeks to break through the enemy's defense and disrupt the defensive system. (Joint Pub 1-02)

persisting: An operational mode in which a military unit attempts to take and hold specific terrain.

phase: A period during which a large portion of the force is involved in similar or mutually supporting activities toward a specific objective. (FM 100-5)

pickets: Out-guards occupying the first line beyond the police guards; when attacked, the outposts and grand guards fall back on the pickets for support. (Gilham)

plan: A continuous, evolving framework for execution that maximizes opportunities—a point of reference rather than a blueprint. (FM 100-5)

planning: The process of putting together a method or schedule of activities directed to accomplishing a specific goal.

pontoons: Small boats used to sustain the bridges across streams for the passage of troops. (Gilham)

priority intelligence requirement: Critical items of information about the enemy and the environment needed by the commander by a certain time to link to available information and intelligence to assist in reaching a logical decision. (FM 100-5)

procedure: A specific documentable event that causes an activity to occur . . . producing a product that normally affects another organization. . . . "what" an organization must do, not "how" it must do it. (Joint Pub 1-02)

protection: Cover or shield from danger. (from Random House)

provost marshal (martial): An officer whose duty it is to see punishments put in force, secure prisoners, etc. (Gilham)

pursuit: An offensive operation designed to catch or cut off a hostile force attempting to escape, with the aim of destroying it. (Joint Pub 1-02)

quartermaster: An officer whose duty it is to supply the quarters, fuel, clothing, transportation, etc., to a body of troops. (Gilham)

raid: An operation, usually small-scale, involving a swift penetration of enemy territory to secure information, confuse the enemy, or to destroy installations. It ends with a planned withdrawal upon completion of the assigned mission. (Joint Pub 1-02)

raiding: An operational mode where a military unit will attack targets in a specific area but will not attempt to hold any specific piece of terrain.

ration: The daily allowance of bread, meat, etc. to the soldiers. (Gilham)

rear guard: Security detachment that protects the rear of a column from hostile forces. During a withdrawal, it delays the enemy by armed resistance, destroying bridges, and blocking roads. (Joint Pub 1-02)

reconnaissance: A mission undertaken to obtain, by visual observation or other detection methods, information about the activities and resources of an enemy or potential enemy, or to secure data concerning the meteorological, hydrographic, or geographic characteristics of a particular area. (Joint Pub 1-02)

redeploy: To transfer a unit, an individual, or supplies deployed in one area to another area, or to another location within the area, or to the zone of the interior for the purpose of further employment. (Joint Pub 1-02)

regiment: A body of troops, composed of ten or twelve companies, and commanded by a colonel. (Gilham)

reinforce: To strengthen with additional men, ships, or aircraft. (Random House)

reserve: Portion of a body of troops which is kept at the rear, or withheld from action at the beginning of an engagement, available for a decisive moment. (Joint Pub 1-02)

resupply: The act of replenishing stocks in order to maintain required levels of supply. (Joint Pub 1-02)

retirement: An operation in which a force out of contact moves away from the enemy. (Joint Pub 1-02)

retrograde: Any movement of a command away from the enemy. (Joint Pub 1-02)

rifle: A shoulder firearm with spiral grooves cut in the inner surface of the gun barrel to give the bullet a rotatory motion and thus render its flight more accurate. (Random House)

risk: Exposure to the chance of injury or loss. (Random House)

sap: A deep, narrow trench leading to an enemy fortification or position. (Random House)

scouting: Employed in reconnoitering. (Random House)

screening force: A security element whose primary mission is to observe, identify, and report information, and which only fights in self protection. (Joint Pub 1-02)

security: Measures taken by a military unit . . . to protect itself against all acts designed to, or which may, impair its effectiveness. (Joint Pub 1-02)

sequel: A future operation that anticipates the outcome of the current operation. (FM 100-5)

siege: The art of surrounding a fortified place with an army, and attacking it by means of batteries, mines, and trenches. (Gilham)

simplicity: The use of uncomplicated concepts and plans and direct, concise orders to ensure thorough understanding. (FM 100-5)

situation: The state of affairs; combination of circumstances. (Random House)

squadron: A . . . cavalry unit consisting of two or more troops, a headquarters, and various supporting units. (Random House)

staff: A body of officers without command authority, appointed to assist a commanding officer. (Random House)

strategic: The level of war at which a nation . . . determines national security objectives and guidance, and develops and uses national resources to accomplish these objectives. (Joint Pub 1-02)

strategy: The art and science of employing the armed forces of the nation or a multinational force to secure policy. (FM 100-5)

supporting attack: An offensive operation carried out in conjunction with a main attack and designed to achieve one or more of the following: a) deceive the enemy; b) destroy or pin down enemy forces which could interfere with the main attack; c) control ground whose occupation by the enemy will hinder the main attack; or d) force the enemy to commit reserves prematurely or in an indecisive area. (Joint Pub 1-02)

surprise: The achieving of effects disproportionate to the effort by taking unexpected action. (FM 100-5)

sustainment: The provision of personnel, logistic, and other support required to maintain and prolong operations or combat until successful accomplishment or revision of the mission or of the national objective. (Joint Pub 1-02)

synchronization: The arrangement of military actions in time, space, and purpose to produce maximum relative combat power at a decisive place and time. (Joint Pub 1-02)

tactics: The art and science of applying capabilities to win battles and engagements or otherwise accomplish tasks and missions. (FM 100-5)

task force: A temporary grouping of units, under one commander, formed for the purpose of carrying out a specific operation or mission. (Joint Pub 1-02)

task organization: The organization of available forces to accomplish a task or mission. Task organization addresses horizontal integration, distributing the combined arms engagement and integrating capabilities to the components of a force. (FM 100-5)

technique: The manner, methods, or ability with which a person fulfills the technical requirements of his particular art or field of endeavor. (Random House)

terrain: A tract of land, especially as considered with reference to its natural features, military advantages, and so on. (Random House)

trains: A service force or group of service elements which provides logistic support; the vehicles and operating personnel which furnish supply, evacuation, and maintenance services to a land unit. (Joint Pub 1-02)

turning movement: A variation of the envelopment in which the attacking force passes around or over the enemy's principal defensive positions to secure objectives deep in the enemy's rear to force the enemy to abandon his position or divert major forces to meet the threat. (Joint Pub 1-02)

uncovered: Not protected. (Random House)

unity-of-effort: The achieving of common purpose and direction through unity of command, coordination, and cooperation. (FM 100-5)

versatility: The ability to perform in many roles and environments, conducting the full range of operations. (FM 100-5)

wargame: A simulation, by whatever means, of a military operation involving two or more opposing forces, using rules, data, and procedures designed to depict an actual or assumed real-life situation. (Joint Pub 1-02)

weather: The state of the atmosphere with respect to wind, temperature, cloudiness, moisture, pressure, and so on. (Random House)

wing: The right or left divisions of an army or battalion. (Gilham)

withdrawal: A planned operation in which a force in contact disengages from an enemy force. (Joint Pub 1-02)

References

GOVERNMENT PUBLICATIONS

Armed Forces Staff College. 1993. AFSC Pub 1, *The Joint Staff Officer's Guide*. Norfolk, Virginia: U.S. Government Printing Office.

Joint Chiefs of Staff. 1995. Joint Pub 5-0, *Doctrine for Planning Joint Operations*. Washington, D.C.: U.S. Government Printing Office.

The Joint Staff. 1994. Joint Pub 1-02, *The DOD Dictionary of Military and Associated Terms*. Washington, D.C.: U.S. Government Printing Office.

———. 1995. Joint Pub 3-0, *Doctrine for Joint Operations*. Washington, D.C.: U.S. Government Printing Office.

Newell, Clayton R. and Michael D. Krause, eds. 1994. *On Operational Art*. Washington, D.C.: United States Army Center of Military History.

U.S. Department of the Army. 1984. Field Manual 101-5, *Staff Organization and Operations*. Washington, D.C.: U.S. Government Printing Office.

———. 1993. Field Manual 100-5, *Operations*. Washington, D.C.: U.S. Government Printing Office.

U.S. War Department. 1880–1901. *The War of the Rebellion: A Compilation of the Official Records of the Union and Confederate Armies*. 128 volumes. Washington, D.C.: U.S. Government Printing Office.

———. 1889–1895. *Atlas to the Official Records of the Union and Confederate Armies*. 3 volumes. Washington, D.C.: U.S. Government Printing Office.

BOOKS

Bode, Frederick A. and Donald E. Ginter. 1986. *Farm Tenancy and the Census in Antebellum Georgia*. Athens, Georgia: The University of Georgia Press.

Castel, Albert. 1992 *Decision in the West: The Atlanta Campaign of 1864*. Lawrence, Kansas: University of Kansas Press.

Connelly, Thomas Lawrence. 1971. *Autumn of Glory: The Army of Tennessee, 1862–1865*. Baton Rouge, Louisiana: Louisiana State University Press.

Cox, Jacob D. 1987. *Atlanta*. Dayton, Ohio: Morningside House, Inc.

Disturnell, J. 1867. *Census of the United States & Territories and of British America; Giving the Population by Counties and Districts, Together with the Cities and Principal Towns; Copied from the Latest Official Census of Both Countries*. New York: The American News Company.

Gilham, Major William. 1861. *Manual of Instruction for the Volunteers and Militia of the United States*. Philadelphia: Charles DeSilver.

Griffith, Paddy. 1986. *Battle in the Civil War*. Camberley, Surrey, England: Fieldbooks.

——. 1989. *Battle Tactics of the Civil War*. New Haven, Connecticut: Yale University Press.

Hagerman, Edward. 1992. *The American Civil War and the Origins of Modern Warfare: Ideas, Organization, and Field Command*. Bloomington, Indiana: Indiana University Press.

Hardee, W. J. 1862. *Hardee's Rifle and Light Infantry Tactics*. New York: J. O. Kane.

Hattaway, Herman and Archer Jones. 1983. *How the North Won: A Military History of the Civil War*. Urbana, Illinois: University of Illinois Press.

Hittle, J. D. 1952. *Jomin and His Summary of the Art of War*. Harrisburg, Pennsylvania: Stackpole Books.

Hooker, Richard D., ed. 1993. *Maneuver Warfare: An Anthology*. Novato, California: Presidio Press.

Johnson, Robert Underwood and Clarence Clough Buel, eds. 1889. *Battles and Leaders of the Civil War: Retreat with Honor*, Volume 4. Secaucus, New Jersey: Castle.

Johnston, Joseph E. 1959. *Narrative of Military Operations During the Civil War*. New York: Da Capo Press, Inc.

Jomini, Baron Antoine Henri. 1854. *Summary of the Art of War*. New York: G. P. Putnam.

Jones, Archer. 1987. *The Art of War in the Western World*. New York: Oxford University Press.

——. 1992. *Civil War Command and Strategy: The Process of Victory and Defeat*. New York: The Free Press.

Leonhard, Robert R. 1991. *The Art of Maneuver: Maneuver Warfare Theory and AirLand Battle*. Novato, California: Presidio Press.

Miles, Jim. 1989. *Fields of Glory: A History and Tour Guide of the Atlanta Campaign*. Nashville, Tennessee: Rutledge Hill Press.

Phillips, T. R. 1955. *Roots of Strategy*. Harrisburg, Pennsylvania: The Military Service Publishing Company.

Price, David P. 1989. *Modern Agriculture*. University Park, New Mexico: SWI Publishing.

Range, Willard. 1954. *A Century of Georgia Agriculture*. Athens, Georgia: The University of Georgia Press.

Scaife, William R. 1993. *The Campaign for Atlanta*. Saline, Michigan: McNaughton & Gunn, Inc.

Sherman, William T. 1984. *Memoirs of General William T. Sherman*. 2 volumes. New York: Da Capo Press, Inc.

Stein, Jess, ed. 1975. *The Random House College Dictionary*, Revised Edition. New York: Random House.

Strayer, Larry M. and Richard A. Baumgartner. 1991. *Echoes of Battle: The Atlanta Campaign*. Huntington, West Virginia: Blue Acorn Press.

Sun Tzu. 1994. *Art of War*. Translated by Ralph D. Summers. Boulder, Colorado: Westview Press.

Symonds, Craig L. 1992. *Joseph E. Johnston: A Civil War Biography*. New York: W. W. Norton & Company.

Thomas, Robert B. 1863. *The (Old) Farmer's Almanack, Calculated on a New and Improved Plan, for the Year of Our Lord 1864*. Boston, Massachusetts: Brewer & Tileston.

Turner, George Edgar. 1992. *Victory Rode the Rails*. Lincoln, Nebraska: University of Nebraska Press.

Von Clausewitz, Carl. 1976. *On War*. Translated by Michael Howard and Peter Paret. Princeton, New Jersey: Princeton University Press.

White, George. 1972. *Statistics of the State of Georgia*. Reprint of the 1849 edition. Savannah, Georgia: W. Thorne Williams.

PERIODICALS AND PROCEEDINGS

Keller, Allan. 1962. "On the Road to Atlanta: Johnston versus Sherman." *Civil War Times Illustrated* 1 (8): 18–22.

Klinger, Michael J. 1989. "Botched Union Attack." *America's Civil War* 12 (3): 20–25.

Luvaas, Jay. 1989. "One or Two Good Spies: Sherman's Use of Intelligence." Fourth USAWC International Conference on Intelligence and Strategy. Carlisle, Pennsylvania.

McMurray, Richard M. 1976. "The Atlanta Campaign of 1864: A New Look." *Civil War History* 22: 5–15.

McMurray, Richard M. 1989. "Atlanta Campaign: Rocky Face to the Dallas Line, the Battles of May 1864." *Blue & Gray Magazine* IV (4). Columbus, Ohio: Blue & Gray Enterprises, Inc.: entire issue.

Moore, John G. 1960. "Mobility and Strategy in the Civil War." *Military Affairs* 24: 68–77.

Tri-Weekly Courier. 1863–4. Rome, Georgia.

MAPS

Brown, Chuck. Undated. "The Atlanta Campaign." Prepared for Pickett's Mill State Historic Site. Scale approximately 1:270,000.

U.S. Geological Survey. 1981. "Atlanta." 1:100,000.

U.S. Geological Survey. 1981. "Cartersville." 1:100,000.

U.S. Geological Survey. 1981. "Chickamauga." 1:100,000.

U.S. Geological Survey. 1981. "Dalton." 1:100,000.

U.S. Geological Survey. 1981. "Rome." 1:100,000.

Index

Note: *Italicized* page numbers indicate illustrations, tables, maps, or photographs; page numbers followed by the letter n refer to an endnote on that page.

About the Author

A NATIVE OF ALABAMA, Brig. Gen. John Scales, AUS (Ret.), served thirty-two years in the Army, the Army National Guard, and the Army Reserve. He spent a year in Vietnam as an infantry platoon leader and assistant operations officer, and he commanded a special operations task force in Afghanistan—with many other military assignments in between. Because twenty-five of his thirty-two years were spent in the Alabama National Guard, primarily in the 20th Special Forces Group (Airborne), he also has a civilian career as an engineer specializing in smart weapons at Science Applications International Corporation. General Scales and his family live in Huntsville, Alabama.

THE NAVAL INSTITUTE PRESS is the book-publishing arm of the U.S. Naval Institute, a private, nonprofit, membership society for sea service professionals and others who share an interest in naval and maritime affairs. Established in 1873 at the U.S. Naval Academy in Annapolis, Maryland, where its offices remain today, the Naval Institute has members worldwide.

Members of the Naval Institute support the education programs of the society and receive the influential monthly magazine *Proceedings* and discounts on fine nautical prints and on ship and aircraft photos. They also have access to the transcripts of the Institute's Oral History Program and get discounted admission to any of the Institute-sponsored seminars offered around the country. Discounts are also available to the colorful bimonthly magazine *Naval History*.

The Naval Institute's book-publishing program, begun in 1898 with basic guides to naval practices, has broadened its scope to include books of more general interest. Now the Naval Institute Press publishes about seventy titles each year, ranging from how-to books on boating and navigation to battle histories, biographies, ship and aircraft guides, and novels. Institute members receive significant discounts on the Press's more than eight hundred books in print.

Full-time students are eligible for special half-price membership rates. Life memberships are also available.

For a free catalog describing Naval Institute Press books currently available, and for further information about subscribing to *Naval History* magazine or about joining the U.S. Naval Institute, please write to:

Member Services
U.S. NAVAL INSTITUTE
291 Wood Road
Annapolis, MD 21402-5034
Telephone: (800) 233-8764
Fax: (410) 571-1703
Web address: *www.navalinstitute.org*